What's Worth

KNOWING

What's Worth
KNOWING

Wendy Lustbader

JEREMY P. TARCHER / PUTNAM
a member of penguin putnam inc.
new york

Jeremy P. Tarcher/Putnam

a member of

Penguin Putnam Inc.

375 Hudson Street

New York, NY 10014

www.penguinputnam.com

Photo Credits: 1–6, 8, 9, 11, 15–22, 25–27, 29, 30, 32–38: Wendy Lustbader.
7, 10, 12–14, 28, 31: Family photograph, used by permission.
23: Art Sill. 24: Lee Ann Reardon. 39: John Freeman.

Library of Congress Cataloging-in-Publication Data

What's worth knowing / [compiled by] Wendy Lustbader.

p.   cm.

ISBN 1-58542-071-9

1. Life.   2. Aged—Interviews.   I. Lustbader, Wendy.   II. Title.

BD431.W454 2001

305.26—dc21   00-060742

Printed in the United States of America

5   7   9   10   8   6

This book is printed on acid-free paper. ∞

Book design by Chris Welch

In memory of my beloved grandmother,

Dorothy Bobrow

Contents

Acknowledgments

My biggest debt of gratitude goes to the people whose words are collected here. Many gave of their wisdom in the hope that it would help me personally lead a better life, never imagining that their words would someday reach a wider audience. To those of you getting to see your words in print, I am happy to give you the satisfaction of having an impact on many other lives. To the friends and relatives of those unable to enjoy this satisfaction, I am pleased to join you in honoring your loved ones.

My agent, Joel Fishman, and my editor, Wendy Hubbert, played major roles by perceiving that this wisdom was worth publishing. I am grateful on many levels for their vision and persistence.

At ProLab, a photographic imaging studio in Seattle, the staff took special care with the photographs, sometimes spending hours on particular negatives in order to arrive at the best prints. Lee Ann Reardon, in particular, helped me select among negatives, suggested the most interesting ways to crop the images, and contributed her creative "feel" to the project in every instance. She also led me to one of the people depicted here, her friend Ben Rail, and contributed a photograph of him.

Others who led me to vivacious older adults are Kathleen Sullivan and John Lester. Readers of the manuscript included Sue Tomita, Orca Giarrusso, Carter Catlett Williams, Jed Kliman, Rose Marie Fagan, and Shirley Crawford, friends whose excitement about the project fed my own. I am especially indebted to Lauren Grosskopf and Valerie Trueblood for the care they took in scrutinizing each vignette, helping me improve the places where I faltered in conveying a speaker's distinctiveness.

Special thanks go to two fellow social workers: Debbie Anderson, who first suggested that I find a way to make this kind of material accessible to all, and Marty Richards, who gave me the assignment that became the genesis of this book.

My husband, Barry Grosskopf, endured too many weekends without companionship and a disproportionate share of household chores in order to ensure that I could put the best of myself into this project. I feel fortunate that our marriage is solid enough for us to continue to hold each other in high regard, despite taking turns disappearing into book writing.

What's Worth

KNOWING

Introduction

My first assignment as a young social work student was to draw out the life stories of the residents of a nursing home, type them up on an old IBM Selectric, and put them in front of the medical charts. The hope was that staff would read these biographies and see beyond a cursory identity to who each person really was.

Shyly, I entered the room of Mrs. Brown, otherwise known as "the lady with the stroke in room 208." She looked dazed, and at first she barely responded to my presence. I pulled up a chair close to her wheelchair and asked where she was from. "Kansas," she said. How long had she been in Seattle? "Since I retired." What had she retired from? "Secretarial work." We both fell silent. It seemed that talking was an effort for her, and I was afraid I was bothering her with my questions.

But my supervisor's instructions were clear. I was to get everyone's life story. Not to fail with my first attempt, I sat back in my chair and started to tell Mrs. Brown about my summer driving cross-country. I bemoaned the seemingly interminable length of Kansas, how I saw nothing but cornfields and wheat fields for hours on end. I speculated about how dull it must be to grow up on a farm with fields as far as the eye can see.

"That's not how it was," she interjected with a strong voice, somewhat indignantly. "We had a lot of fun." She told me about her sisters and brothers, how they all ran around freely, unlike the kids in cities and suburbs today whose parents must confine them for their own safety. "We were in our own world," she declared. "We chased butterflies, made up adventures, dug in the dirt—we didn't stop playing for a minute, from dawn to dusk." She told me about the winter snows that sometimes trapped all of them happily at home for a week away from school. She became more and more animated, describing the warm bricks from the fireplace that were put under quilts for the long, cold nights, and the smell of the bread her mother would bake all day, once a week, in the huge woodstove in her kitchen.

A few hours went by. We were both enchanted, she with the rush of memories and I with the sense of moving back in time to a way of life that had vanished. We stopped only because it was time for lunch. She grabbed my hand when I stood up to leave and said, "No one has listened to me like that in years."

Not every person in the nursing home was as articulate as she, nor as able to recount the past with such vividness, but everyone I spoke with had something to say. Even the people with Alzheimer's had pockets of memory still available to them, often from their distant youth, and would launch into their stories with gusto. I began asking questions like, "If you could live your life over, what would you do differently?" or "What advice would you give a young person who is trying to live a good life?" I was truly interested in hearing their answers. Most people replied with enthusiasm and often with pithy insights about living well. Gratefully, I went home and preserved these in the personal journal I'd been keeping since grade school.

The assignment to listen to the stories of older people had opened up a world of unexpected richness to me. I decided to concentrate on gerontology for the rest of my time in social work school, which meant attending seminars with only three or four fellow students. Classes and field placements on youth and family counseling were mobbed, but I was the only applicant to my second-year placement in the geriatric unit of a hospital. There I sat at the bedsides of older people on the verge of going to nursing homes or pleading for one more try at making it at home. I had less time to hear life stories, but lots to learn about tenacity and maintaining dignity against all odds.

I became a geriatric social worker, taking a job with an agency called Visiting Nurses immediately after graduation. My duties consisted of visiting my patients in their homes and mustering up enough supportive services to keep them there. One of my favorite patients was a retired businessman in his late seventies, laid low by emphysema, who delighted in describing his many hours watching cloud formations emerge and disappear: "There're so many things you can see in the sky. You make sculptures with your imagination." As a younger man, he said, an afternoon spent like this would have been unimaginable. Yet these had been some of the best afternoons of his life.

From this man, I began to see how physical limitations can lead to expansion in other realms, such as the imagination and the spirit. Sadly, in our society infirmities of the body are frequently equated with weaknesses of the mind. Young and old typically have little but superficial contact with each other. We let appearances deceive us and dismiss what our elders have to teach us even before we give them a chance to speak. Thus, we forfeit the wisdom accumulated through lifetimes.

During this time, I became friends with a ninety-eight-year-old woman who lived in a nursing home. Despite our close relationship, she insisted that I go on calling her Mrs. Chittick, rather than Edna, because I was "impossibly young." I spent three wonderful years with her before she died in 1984 at the age of one hundred and one. She was a window into another century, describing how at the age of twenty-nine she had run to the top of a hill to see her first automobile. She never flew in an airplane, but she had crossed the Atlantic four times by ship, once to study piano in Paris. She never so much as touched a computer keyboard, but her gnarled fingers often tapped out a Schubert piano sonata on the arm of her wheelchair. She never had children, but she nurtured her piano students like kin. Their loving letters flowed in faithfully till the day she died. Her vision was poor, so I read these letters and her favorite poetry aloud to her as we enjoyed a glass of sherry. She showed me how the power to attract friendship need never atrophy, even if eyesight, dexterity, and the ability to walk are long gone.

Over the next two decades, I spent most of my work life with people in their seventies, eighties, nineties, and older. All along, I was aware of being among the privileged few who had crossed a societal barrier. Using terms like "the elderly," we tend to keep older people separate from ourselves. We shirk the obvious but uncomfortable reality that older people are just people who have gotten older. The truth is, we become more ourselves as we get older, more individuated, less similar to our chronological peers.

One day, an idea took hold of me—I would consult my journals and assemble into a book the best of what I had learned from older people. The bounty I had gathered would then be available to others. *What's Worth Knowing* contains vignettes from older people I met in my work, but also from family members, friends, and people I met by chance on street corners and trains. I have tried to keep each piece as close as possible to the sentiment each person revealed to me, although these accounts—by necessity—are not verbatim transcripts. Half-completed thoughts, dangling tangents, and circumlocutions, easily tolerated in face-to-face conversation, are infuriating on the page.

As I proceeded to record these legacies of wisdom, I became aware that too much editing could take the life out of the vignettes. There was nuance and intimation in each person's manner of expression, meaning that could be heard between the lines. There were instances where the speech verged on being trite or hackneyed, but the undertones were profound. Gradually, the chief paradox in this work emerged: that a certain amount of craft would be necessary to get closest to what is recognizable as real. Through successive drafts, the vignettes became more and more true to life. I came to see that the same principles of condensation inherent in fiction were vital here.

Are these vignettes real? Yes. Are they verbatim renderings? No. Do they sound like the people who spoke them? Yes. Did I alter the spirit of what was said? No. Did I shape the vignettes to make them more readable? Certainly. A model for this book was *Spoon River Anthology* by Edgar Lee Masters, published in 1915. His was a fictional collection of epitaphs based on people he had known. Mine is a nonfiction assemblage of what real people said, employing techniques of fiction.

When possible, I have gone back to the speaker with his or her contribution, asking, "Does this sound like you?" In other instances, I brought a similar question to the person's surviving friend or relative. Edits and rewrites arrived in the mail, and the vignettes became more accurate still. In every case where a photograph appears, the real name of the person has been used. Other names are pseudonyms either because the person asked not to be named or the person is deceased and relatives could not be located. I took most of the photographs during conversations, using an old Canon with natural lighting.

Certain themes emerged as I compiled the vignettes, despite the diversity of age, background, and personal circumstance of the speakers. These themes became the book's eleven sections: on living well, on people, on time, on spirituality, on marriage, on being blue, on work, on illness and frailty, on good conduct, on regret, and on later life. Despite disagreeing with each other at times, the speakers converge in their regard for what they consider worth knowing.

On the morning of his hundredth birthday, a man named Henry sat alone in a suit and tie as he waited patiently in the lobby of his retirement home for the arrival of the mayor of Seattle and a battery of TV cameras. While he waited, he told me about his experiences as a sailor in the South Pacific in 1915, long before radar allowed sailors to peer through fog. He described being rescued by another ship during a storm, having only one chance to jump from his wildly pitching ship to the other, which he could barely see. Henry had a great deal to say about leaps he had taken since, during his many subsequent years of hardy living. He spoke with such flair and animation that I kept wondering, "Why aren't scores of people lined up to talk to this man?"

In the following pages, I invite you to sit beside people like Henry. I think you will see, as I have, that there is nothing sweeter than being able to live the middle of one's life with the perspective of the end.

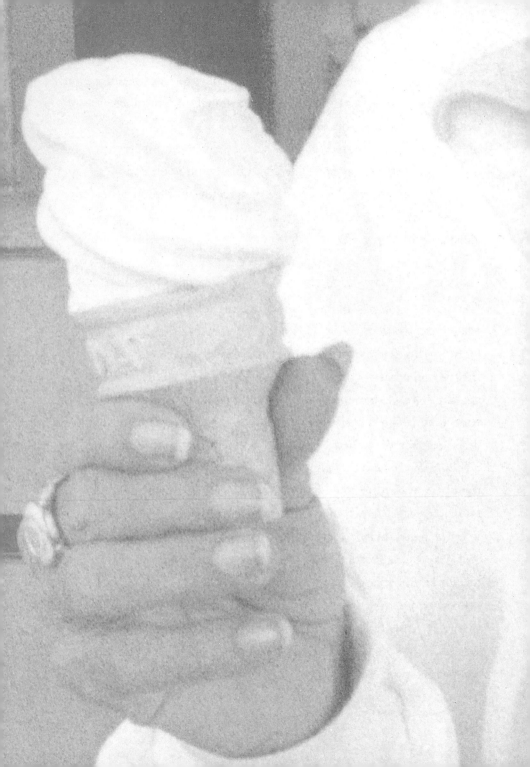

On
Living Well

You don't need much.

IRMA DELEHANTY

Age 72

We lost everything during the depression, except for the family. We held together. A lot of times we were barely making it, but we could always go for walks with each other or somebody would get a song going for us all to sing. Doing simple things together as a family made us happy. These days, wealth and success is what people strive for, and—believe me—I'm not knocking it. But what I learned as a kid has never failed me.

After she was diagnosed with cancer, Irma Delehanty had a few years to say what needed to be said to her loved ones and to receive the affection they were eager to express. To her son, Ron, she confided the hope that she was teaching him how to die well. She lived those last years with her typical vivaciousness. This ice cream cone was savored just a month or so before she died.

You've got to keep a sense of humor.

ROSIE BARLOW MILLS

Age 90

*S*eeing what's funny, even in a terrible situation, is the only way to live. I learned this from my grandmother. She took care of me when I came down with polio at the age of nine. One day we were driving in one of those early model cars, half open at the sides, and I had a leg spasm. I started sliding down off the seat. My grandmother leaned over and grabbed me and pulled me back up, but meanwhile she plowed right into a telephone pole. The car was a mess. People came over to help us and she told them, "At least I kept her on the seat."

Bill and I were married almost seventy years, short by just two weeks. On the day he died, he asked me to get into bed with him. He was cold. He wanted me to put my arms around him and warm him up. So, as I was climbing into the bed, I said, "Bill, that sounds like a proposition." Without missing a beat, he answered, "I wish to God it was." That was the last thing he ever said to me. I smile whenever I think of it.

A flair for telling a good story sustained Rosie Barlow Mills through many travails in her old age. The polio she overcame as a child resurfaced when she was in her eighties, and it often caused her to lose her balance. One winter morning, she went out to retrieve the newspaper, but fell into a snowbank and could not get back up. While waiting for her husband to find her, she entertained herself by imagining how she would tell the story of her morning in the snowbank, slowly freezing into the shape of a twisted old lady with a broken wrist.

Kindness is never wasted.

AGNES MCDOUGAL

Age 98

I can't believe I am almost a hundred, and I can still tell you things that happened when I was a little girl. I remember that grumpy old farmer who lived up our lane. I can still hear him yelling at us when my brothers and sister and I cut across his land on the way to school. But in the dead of winter, when the snow was too deep for any shortcut, there he was, coming down the lane with his wagon, making sure we got to school before we froze to death.

You remember things like that, people who were good to you. When I was seventeen, leaving home for the first time, I was sitting on a train across from an old lady. We were held up in Chicago, just sitting there for a long time. I was starving. The lady suddenly reached into her bag and handed me an apple. To this day, I can still taste that apple.

The nursing home bed rails restrained Agnes McDougal's body but her mind moved with agility through her past, especially her Kansas childhood. She simply needed a listener to get her going, and then she was off in realms that required no further prompting. A question about the corn harvest led to her recalling her mother baking bread for farmhands, and this brought her to the pleasure of running out into the fields at midmorning with a basketful of muffins to bring to the men.

Happiness is in the smallest things.

BERNICE MILLER
Age 61

When I was thirty, I was in a wicked car accident. For nine months I was stuck in a body cast, chest to my toes. I didn't know you could be that miserable. I wanted to die. I begged my sister to give me an overdose of morphine. She wouldn't. Instead, she pulled me out of the hospital and stuck me in her basement, the only room with a bathroom right there. Her friends came down to gawk at me, like something from an archaeological dig. I was a sight! What stuck out of the cast at both ends was dark purple. I would have given anything to be able to go to the bathroom on my own—to have sweet, sweet privacy! To scratch anywhere I wanted! To feel a breeze on my skin!

Ever since that time, I've hardly ever been depressed. I appreciate every little freedom, because I still remember what it was like not to be able to do those things.

Bernice Miller told me the story of her car wreck on the way to a hotel from the airport, minutes after we met for the first time in a shuttle van. She narrated every detail of the accident and the aftermath, especially when a traffic jam on the freeway granted the tale an unhurried pace. Along the way, she also commented on the van's comfortable plush seats, the courtesy of the driver, and the golden color of the late afternoon light on the trees beside the road.

Learn to like your own company.

ANNIE BAKERSMITH

Age 97

I always needed to have people around me. That's how I was. Something had to be going on all the time. If I was by myself, even for a little while, I'd get restless. I was out the door before you could blink. I'd rather do anything than be alone.

But then I got to a certain age. Until then, I never knew that you could run out of people to see and places to go. My friends started dying off, and I wasn't able to drive at night anymore. It got to be there was nothing to do, and nobody to come over. I got stuck with my own company.

At first, I hated it. Imagine getting acquainted with yourself at eighty! It's better to learn how to get along on your own when you're young. Later, the only one you can count on for company is yourself. I'm starting to get a kick out of it now, but solitude takes practice.

Annie Bakersmith always answered the knock at her door with enthusiasm, especially if it was time for afternoon tea. She would set out her Royal Albert teacups with the matching cream and sugar set, along with fancy silver spoons on handsome linen napkins. A plate full of delicate cookies with layers of chocolate was always placed in the center of her kitchen table, as if awaiting a throng of inevitable guests. The truth was, only a few people ever knocked on Annie's door.

Things you buy won't make you happy.

MAXINE DOUGHERTY

Age 81

My mother never stood for any whining. If I wanted a certain pair of shoes or a special dress I'd seen in a shop window, she'd say, "You think that will make you happy? Then save your money and go out and get it." So, I'd save and save for the longest time, and then go get myself that pair of shoes or that dress. I'd feel so good coming in the house and flaunting my bag from the store. I'd put my loot on the couch and show it off there all day, looking at it, touching it, trying it on over and over again. After a day or two, the thrill would be gone, but I was already planning my next shopping expedition.

I can tell you now my mother was right, but it took me so many years and so much money down the drain before I stopped trying to prove her wrong. You just don't find happiness through buying things—not for long, anyway.

Maxine Dougherty's self-deprecating humor and overall modesty made it hard for me to believe that she had once been a princess, her term for her earlier self. She was embarrassed to recall how her material desires had far outweighed other aims and had led her to marry a "despicable" man for his money. Her life story was a fairy tale in reverse. She didn't turn into a toad at the end, but rather a contented person unencumbered by desires beyond her humble means.

There's always something to see, if you keep your eyes open.

LILA LANE

Age 77

I love color. I have to have it. I love paints, crayons, pastels, markers, ink, the wilder the better. I have to be making something all the time, and making something of myself. Otherwise, life is too drab.

I go down to the clinic and help out. It doesn't matter what I do there—stuff envelopes, put labels on folders, whatever they need done. All the while, I'm watching the show. The staff run around, the patients try to get what they want. Everybody's doing their thing, and I've got a front-row seat. That's how I keep myself going. I have no sympathy for the ones that sit home complaining that they have no life. There's a whole world out here, if you bother to look.

At age sixteen, Lila Lane ran off to Tijuana to marry her first husband. She had a string of marriages after that, while working a wide variety of jobs, from telephone operator to casino dealer to barmaid. In the last few years of her life, she was a beloved volunteer at the medical clinic where I work. Once or twice a week, she would come to the clinic wearing moccasins and knee-high hose under her slacks, all the while bemoaning the fact that she could no longer wear high heels. When asked why she would never wear socks no matter what the weather, she replied, "Socks make my feet look too big."

Be good to your parents—someday you may understand them.

JACK MELNICK
Age 68

I kept my grudges against my parents long after they were gone. Then, when I was fifty-six, my business went bad. It was a combination of bad luck and bad decisions. There I was, almost bankrupt, just when my youngest kid was starting college. I had to pull her out of school. She's been blaming me ever since for messing up her life.

She won't listen to my side of the story, just like I wouldn't with my parents. I want to tell her, "Hey, I'm doing my best. Sometimes things don't work out the way you want them to." But she couldn't care less, just like me at that age. I sure hope I live long enough to see her respect me again.

In later years, many people describe coming to peace with resentments toward their parents. Jack Melnick once dreamt that he was talking to his father, telling him all the things that had happened since he died and how sorry he was not to have heeded more of his advice when he was alive.

Make sure you go to Paris.

BETTY SEVILLE

Age 76

I always wanted to go to Paris. Harry would say, "Wait till next year. Wait till the kids are done with college. Wait till after we get a new roof." Wait, wait, wait, that's all I ever heard. Then he went and had his stroke, not a week after he retired.

You'll always have plenty of reasons for putting things off. Waiting makes good sense at the time. But later you'll see things differently. Trust me.

Instead of living her dreams of travel, Betty Seville found herself cooped up in her house for six months, tending to her paralyzed husband. She couldn't get him down the steps to their car, and their front yard was too small to install a wheelchair ramp. Even going to the movies with him became as unattainable as going to Paris.

Don't let doubt in yourself defeat you.

ROCKY ADAMS
Age 72

You compete against yourself, not anybody else. Don't look over your shoulder at others. Don't let me see you looking at the birds, or at the pennies on the ground. Look straight ahead and focus. You never know what you can do—not until you do it. You've got to concentrate on your own effort, and aim further than you think you can reach.

As a track coach, Rocky Adams was known to be tough, refusing to patronize his runners with false praise or easy encouragement. He came down hard on those who did not give their best, but he also noticed every personal triumph out on the track. Whether the team won or lost, Rocky was on the lookout for the victories that mattered.

On
People

All that matters is whether someone is a good person.

ISRAEL GROSSKOPF
Age 83

What impresses you? Fancy clothes? A smooth talker? A big shot? It's all garbage. It can all go in a minute. When I was in hiding during the war, it was always a question of who you could trust. Would that one let you hide in his barn? Would he betray you for a piece of bread? That was it.

I never got much school, but I can still tell you who's who. A professor isn't better than a bricklayer. The bricklayer might give you a drink of water when you pass him on the road, while the professor turns his back.

Israel Grosskopf survived the war in Nazi Europe by fleeing east, first joining the Russian army, then deserting to the forests and villages of Siberia. He lived by his wits and often had to depend on the kindness of strangers. He became a good judge of people, because there were many instances when he had to decide whether or not someone was worthy of his trust. After the war, he made a new life in the United States with his wife and son, always relying on his eye for who was a good person and who was not.

Everyone needs a little praise.

HARRY McINTOSH
Age 67

In my house growing up, not a kind word was ever spoken. My father didn't want us to get a big head. He thought he should toughen us up, especially us boys. The girls at least got a pat on the back when he was in the mood, but he was gruff with them, too. If he caught our mother being nice to us, he'd let her have it. He had the meanest tongue you ever heard.

I've dedicated my whole life to being the opposite of him. I go out of my way to praise people. I was the most popular supervisor in my company. Everyone wanted to be transferred to my department, and I got good work out of my people. I don't care how tough someone acts—even someone who shows no reaction is glad to hear appreciation.

The day of his official retirement, Harry McIntosh started volunteering as a crossing guard for his local school district. He told me how much fun it was for him to talk to the kids as they waited to cross the street: "Some of them need a little cheering up, so I try to put a smile on their faces. I figure they come from households like the one I grew up in."

No one's better than you, and you're not better than anyone.

AGNES WILSON

Age 94

I wasted a lot of my life envying other people. But nobody has a perfect life. If you get to know people up close, you see their warts.

We're all basically the same. Even the most confident people have doubts, and the most financially successful people have insecurities. I wish I had realized this seventy years ago, instead of worrying all the time that everyone else's grass was greener than mine. It's a relief when you finally figure it out.

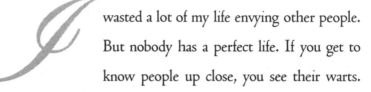

Around the turn of the previous century, Agnes Wilson's father sold rags and other odds and ends out of a wagon. She grew up using pages from the Sears catalog as toilet paper, and wore cast-off clothes from wealthy cousins when she was lucky enough to fit into them. It took her the greater part of a lifetime to stop comparing her circumstances to the idealized lives of others.

A good listener is someone who's not talking.

HAROLD JONES
Age 76

The average person is only interested in his own feelings and his immediate surroundings. The exceptional person always wants to learn about the world outside his own backyard.

You already know all about yourself, so why think about yourself all the time? You should ask questions and really pay attention to the answers. Try on someone else's life. And if you're shy, don't worry. Almost everyone likes to talk. People will tell you everything, especially on buses and trains. The longer you're trapped together, the better. People really let loose. You'll get quite an education.

Harold Jones lived in a senior high-rise building with a hundred resi-
dents, ninety-six of them women. The three other men were reclusive.
He never had a free moment.

Fools are in this world to make us grow.

CHRISTINA MARTINEZ

Age 75

You shouldn't go around complaining this one's a fool and that one's a fool. They're everywhere, and you should be glad. You'd be nowhere without the fools. They show you how you don't want to be.

While they're busy acting like dolts, watch what they're doing. Even if they drive you crazy, study them carefully, then take a good look at yourself. See if you're doing any of those same things. That's what makes you do better.

Be grateful they're making the mistakes, not you. That's what fools are here for. They save you a lot of time and energy.

Christina Martinez sat for hours each afternoon in the lobby of the busy downtown building where she lived, taking up her post in the far corner shortly after lunch. Dramas erupted every day among the other residents, a mix of mentally ill people trying out life on their own, drug addicts beginning their recovery, and physically disabled people like herself. Whenever I had the time to sit next to her, I found her vantage point as edifying as she claimed—a parade of people flaunting their foibles for all to see, sometimes heroically but often foolishly.

It's not going to get better until we stop passing it back and forth.

GLADYS KENNEBREW

Age 71

I'm sorry to say it, but there's still lots of prejudice in the world. I grew up in the South, so I've been through plenty. But I don't believe in teaching your children hate. I taught mine respect, no matter what somebody's color. Stopping the cycle of hate is the only way we're going to get somewhere.

Gladys Kennebrew was born in Louisiana at a time when it was still legal to discriminate because of the color of one's skin. She married, moved to the Pacific Northwest, and raised three sons and two daughters. She taught her children to conduct themselves with decency. Times have changed, but for Gladys the lessons of decency have always been the same.

Take care of yourself, because no one else will.

GEORGE W. HINDELS
Age 80

*S*ure people can be nice. But when things go bad, the veneer of civilization goes in a hurry. People become worse than animals when they feel threatened. Someone you thought was a friend will turn against you. People are basically out for themselves.

My grandchildren are too trusting. I'm trying to warn them, but not make them feel badly about other people. I want them to be more realistic. You can't go around with your head in the clouds. Good or bad, people are what they are, and there are times when you can't count on anyone else to look out for you. It's better all around if you never forget this.

George W. Hindels was born in Vienna, Austria, in 1914. In 1939 he was arrested and taken to a concentration camp. Luckily, a visa that he had applied for seven years before came through, and he was allowed to leave for the United States. He worked his way through dental school, married, and raised two children. He lived a full life, but never forgot the bitter lessons of his youth.

Remember that flesh is weak.

IRENE MUNKBERG

Age 91

I ask you, why would someone go out at night and leave her husband home alone with a single woman? I don't care if it's her cousin or her best friend. Why create situations of temptation? A man and a woman alone in a house—what do you expect? Human beings are not made of steel.

Now, don't go calling me sexist or giving me that modern claptrap about egalitarian relationships. It's not enough to be sophisticated—you've got to be smart.

Human vulnerability was Irene Munkberg's favorite topic. She brandished her insights with so much flair that I would never fail to leave her house both convinced and forewarned.

Living things need lots of attention.

GIUSEPPE MAESTRIAMI

Age 85

I don't care if the whole neighborhood thinks I am a crazy old man. "There's that old fool who talks to his tomato plants, who dotes on them all day long." Let them laugh. My tomatoes always turn out to be the best on the block.

I touch my plants. I make sure they have plenty to drink. I pinch off the extra leaves, but I leave a few for a little shade on the hot days. Sure, I talk to them. Why not? Tending a garden isn't so different from raising children. Plants like when you spend time with them. My kids turned out pretty good, too.

Another thing. Don't keep the whole crop for yourself. There's always people who don't know how to make things grow, and they need your tomatoes more than anybody else.

Between May and October, Giuseppe Maestriami could always be found in his garden, sitting on a low stool among his plants. Occasionally, he would reach too zealously for a weed and topple over. He'd lie there, breathing in the smell of soil and greenery, until his son came home from work to rescue him, or he'd sometimes crawl to a spot where his predicament was visible to passersby. Even during the dormancy of winter, he fed his compost bin faithfully with kitchen scraps, proud that nothing in his life was wasted.

Good fortune is having good friends.

JOHN CAUGHLAN

Age 89

Your family is stuck with you. After you get married, your wife is stuck with you, too. But friends are free to come and go. The ones who stay by your side become your treasures. They just plain *like* you.

I'm proud of certain things I've done in my life, certain accomplishments. But look at my friends. You can't just go out and acquire them. You make them. Years go by, and you go through hard times together. It takes some doing. I look around and see how lucky I am to have such fine people in my life.

As a lawyer, John Caughlan fought for social justice all of his life. Arguing cases before the Supreme Court, he often took up causes that paid him only in satisfaction. He went to court many times on behalf of a Canadian friend the government was trying to deport because of her ties to the Communist Party. By the time he was in his eighties and she was in her nineties, more than forty years later, the struggle was finally over—they had outlived their adversaries. More than his host of professional accomplishments, his loving family, and the wide circle of people who admired him, he was most proud of his friendships. The day before he went into a coma from which he never emerged, he smiled up from his pillow on his hospital bed and reveled in what he regarded as his greatest fortune.

On Time

Knowing you're going to die — that's what really gets you moving.

ARSENE ST. AMAND
Age 48

You can go through a whole lot of years wasting time. You can go down lots of wrong roads. You say, "Hey, I'll take care of that next year." You're too busy showing everyone how much you've got it together. Then—boom—there isn't much time left.

Most people find out about love when they're young, but I didn't. I thought I could do without it. But as soon as the doctor said, "You've got nine months," that was it. I was done fooling around. I decided—before I die, I'm going to learn how to love.

Arsene St. Amand grew up on the streets of New Orleans and went to school only until third grade. He never learned how to write, but in the last year of his life he dictated many letters to those he wanted to thank for having helped him earlier on. Arsene died at the age of forty-eight of lung cancer, shortly after marrying Rose, the love of his life. Dying young, he felt, had made him old inside and wiser than his years.

A long past is a fine possession.

PEARL AIKEN
Age 86

They say it's bad to live in the past. But what if you've had an interesting life? Maybe you like going back over it. Is that so terrible? For some reason, we're always patting young people on the back, congratulating them, "You've got your whole life in front of you." But since when is it better to look forward than to look back?

No one applauds when most of your life is behind you, but I say they should. We should be proud of having a long past. The future is just a guess.

Pearl Aiken declared the benefits of her long past with such confidence that I began to feel proud of approaching my fifth decade, rather than anxious. She emanated nothing but celebration regarding the accrual of years well lived.

Be careful, or machines will take over your life.

ETHEL BAINBRIDGE
Age 90

When I was a girl, telephones were an entirely different affair than they are now. It used to mean something when the phone rang. Now it could be just anything, or nothing at all. It used to be you had a purpose when you used the telephone—to reach the doctor, to arrange a journey, that sort of thing. It certainly wasn't for casual conversation. Other families shared the line, anyway, so you never knew who was listening in.

Now people stay on the phone for hours at a time. Visitors have to sit there like dummies when the host jumps up to get a phone call. I think the machines are in charge now and the people are slaves. As soon as they walk in the door, they run straight over to the answering machine to see who called. Some of them even have phones ringing in their pockets or purses. I don't see how they get any peace.

After Ethel Bainbridge had a stroke, her daughter insisted she move in with the family during her recuperation. She watched their lives in astonishment. The telephone separated them from each other in the evenings, yet they didn't seem to mind. Ethel worries that after her generation dies off, we will forget that it is possible for families to spend evenings together without distraction.

Your days aren't worthless just because you're idle.

EFFIE BRAMFIELD

Age 81

I always had to be accomplishing something. I'm talking about every minute of every day, sunup to sundown. That's how I was brought up. There were no idle hands in our house. Raising my family, a day was wasted unless I sewed a dress and put up a week's worth of soup and darned a dozen socks. Then I did all this all over again, helping my daughter raise her family.

Now I'm an old lady and my hands are knotted up with arthritis. There's hardly anything I can work on anymore. I used to wander around the house, muttering "useless hands, useless life." I certainly couldn't sit on a couch and say it was a good day.

Lately, I've decided to stop fighting it. I've been letting my mind roam while my hands rest. You know what I'm thinking now? There's not a thing wrong with sitting still. You just have to relax into it.

Like many from her background and generation, Effie Bramfield found herself adrift in the open time of later life without feeling free to accept its benefits. No matter how often she was reassured that it was fine to be unproductive, that she deserved to rest at long last, she'd still browbeat herself for getting so little done every day. Ever so gradually, she began to let herself be.

It's good to stay put.

BO JACKSON

Age 81

I was born in Springfield. I was married in Springfield. I'm going to die in Springfield. That's the way I want it. The mayor went to elementary school with my son, I'll have you know, and my daughter baby-sat for the postmaster's kids. Every single family on this block remembers getting a plate of fresh-baked cookies from me when they first moved in. You should've seen when I broke my hip. Everybody in the neighborhood rushed over to give me a hand. I never spend a holiday alone, even when my kids can't get out here.

Young people think someplace else is always better, but they're wrong. Where nobody knows you, you're nothing. Putting lots of time into a place—years and years—that's what makes you count for something.

Somewhere between Middletown, Connecticut, and Springfield, Massachusetts, Bo Jackson sat down next to me on the bus and began recounting the major events of her life. She finished her story right before disembarking in Springfield, the place where she said her grave site was already paid for and the stone had already been ordered.

Make your days worth remembering.

BILL MILTON
Age 89

There's two kinds of people—the ones who live hard and the ones who take it easy. The hard livers are tough on themselves. They take chances. They never stay comfortable for too long. The easy livers play it safe. They never push themselves. One year runs into the next, because the years are all basically the same.

To youngsters, I say, live hard. This is your one and only life, the only show in town. You can't get any of your days back. Live as if you're going to be old someday, looking back on everything you did. It's everything you *didn't* do that will bug the heck out of you.

Bill Milton spent all his working life as a public school janitor and handyman. He loved having the summers off, when he would fashion himself a unique adventure each year. Alone, he would travel to someplace he'd never been and take his tent deep into the woods. After he retired, arthritis made these long treks uncomfortable, but he had already hiked on every continent, in every kind of terrain. He told me that staying home now was OK with him, because he had so many days worth remembering.

Take the time, while you have it.

HENRY ASHTON

Age 92

People today are rushing around, driving themselves crazy. I've never seen so much rushing. No one has any time anymore. What happened to time? In my day, we had time. Now everybody's so busy packing it all in, they don't have any.

You don't have to wait till you go to the Himalayas. Go stand outside in your backyard and listen to the birds. I'm telling you, the time is there to be had. It's there for you every day. You don't have to wait till you're on vacation. Before you know it, you'll be ninety-two.

Henry Ashton was fond of quoting Henry David Thoreau's essay on the delights one can apprehend in one's backyard. This became especially important to him after a stroke took out a major portion of his visual field and he had to give up driving. The one liability he had trouble adapting to was his tendency to walk into objects in his blind spot, such as trees, bushes, and his wife as she crouched in her garden.

How time goes is up to you.

ANNA ORNISH
Age 81

When I was little, a day seemed to last forever, especially a school day. Now a day is nothing, just the blink of an eye. You know intellectually that a month is still a month, a week is a week, a day is a day, but it goes so much faster the older we get.

Sometimes I play a little game with myself. I know it's odd, but I do it just the same. I try to make time pass like it did when I was a child. First, I shut off the television and listen to the ticking of the clock. That slows everything down. Then I tell my worries to back off so I can concentrate. It works like a charm. The morning lasts a long, long time.

Anna Ornish had never been exposed to Eastern meditation tech-niques, but when I told her that some of what she was doing had been taught in traditions a few thousand years old, she said, "Good. That means I'm not so peculiar."

Picturing the world without yourself in it is good for your health.

SEAN O'CALLAHAN

Age 68

planted a maple tree next to the first house I owned, just a skinny runt of a thing. That's all I could afford at the time. It seemed far off in the future before that tree would amount to anything. But when I went back there forty years later, I couldn't believe my eyes. That tree was towering over the house, the queen of the neighborhood.

In the meantime, I'd become an old man. Next to that tree's existence, my brief lifetime hardly amounted to anything. This was the first time I ever really believed that the world will go on just fine after I'm gone. Ever since then, I've been living in tree time. It's a fine way to live.

Sean O'Callahan insisted that the world would be a better place if we all steeped ourselves in the awareness of how trees continue to grow more sturdy as we become more frail. "Then we would all be properly humbled," he declared.

Spirituality

God will take care of it.

NATE PORTER
Age 84

e were the only black family in town. My great-grandmother, Lucinda Shelby, had moved the family up to eastern Washington from the South to get us out of poverty. She herself had been a slave, born in 1842. She was a house slave, rather than a field slave, but still a slave. Grandma Shelby and my grandmother raised me because my mother died when I was a baby and my father was crippled in a train accident.

When I'd walk to school, the white kids threw rocks at me. I asked my Grandma Shelby, "What should I do when they throw rocks at me and call me names?" She said not to worry, God will take care of it. Well, I got pretty good at throwing a hook shot with flat river stones. The stone is hard to dodge, looking like it's coming from someplace else. I launched a few, thinking of David and Goliath, and those kids learned to leave me be.

Later, in Seattle, I was the first black man that made ship-

74

wright in the union, and that opened the door for others. Grandma Shelby was right. She died while I was still in high school, but I've tried to live by her faith all my life.

Nate Porter wished that young people today knew how hard his generation fought for equal rights. As a marine carpenter, he watched for years as white men with less experience got promoted to journeyman while he stayed stuck on the bottom rung, a mere assistant. One day out on the docks, promotions were being announced and he couldn't take it anymore. "What about me?" he bellowed. All fell silent. Everyone knew he deserved a promotion. That day, he became a journeyman carpenter, breaking the color line for himself and all who came after him.

All the beauty in life is right in front of you.

MARTHA McCALLUM
Age 86

One morning I was sitting at my kitchen table, staring into space. It was one of those windy days when the sun keeps coming out and going in. All of a sudden, a sunbeam crossed my kitchen table and lit up my crystal saltshaker. There were all kinds of colors and sparkles. It was one of the most beautiful sights I'd ever seen.

But you know, that very same saltshaker had been on that kitchen table for over fifty years. Surely there must have been other mornings when the sun crossed the table like that, but I was just too busy getting things done. I wondered what else I'd missed. I realized this was it, this was grace.

Once arthritis slowed her down, Martha McCallum would spend a lot of time sitting at her kitchen table. She had such a fully alive presence that to those who joined her at the table she herself seemed to gleam as much as her crystal saltshaker.

Live right, while you can.

EDWARD DAVIS

Age 57

Man, did I used to run around! I smoked and drank and drugged like there was no tomorrow. I had everything—money, women, cars, houses, you name it. So it was a big shock when I got sick and lost it all.

Every day now I pray, "Please give me back my health. I promise to live right." I'm praying hard. If I could get strong enough, I'd take a cab to the schools around here and show those young people what could happen if they don't quit messing around with the cigarettes, the booze, and everything else. It seems that letting the kids see me like this is the best way I can serve God.

Edward Davis asked that his photograph and real name not be used in this book because his mother does not yet know he is hooked up to an oxygen tank. She would be upset to realize just how ill he has become at such a young age. He, too, still has a hard time accepting his condition, insisting on going without his oxygen to get his groceries. Though he gasps for breath every few aisles, these outings give him a few hours each week to walk in the world as if he is well.

It's not your place to know the answers.

FRANK BONEKAMP

Age 79

For months I was in pain all the time, night and day. Lots of times I was up all night long. I kept asking God, what did I do that was so terrible? I haven't been perfect, but I've certainly been decent. Why do I have to be punished like this?

One night, I was really furious, really ranting and raving at God for my suffering. Then it hit me. I was acting just like Job. Who was I to ask God all these questions? Am I supposed to be God's equal? A great peace came over me. It was four-thirty in the morning. My pain got better. It got so still and quiet. My mind stopped making all that noise.

Frank Bonekamp was stricken with an unusually painful form of multiple sclerosis. Medicines did not seem to diminish his suffering, and he would often cry out so loudly in the night that he woke up his neighbors in adjoining apartments. It was the Book of Job that relieved him in ways that painkillers could not. He still suffered until the release of death, but not in the same way, and never again to such depths.

God acts through you, not for you.

GERALD HUNTLEY

Age 62

I can't stand people who sit around waiting for God to get them what they want, as if God's got nothing better to do. They complain about their lot in life, how they don't have this or don't have that.

I don't have much sympathy for that kind of talk. I'd rather hear what you've done lately for someone else, or what steps you've taken to get out of the pickle you're in. You've got to do your part. You have to make some kind of an effort. That's the divine in us—making use of the gifts we are given.

Gerald Huntley has been blind since birth. He is acutely aware of his difference from others, but he doesn't refer to it and feels he does not miss a capacity that he never possessed. Gerald literally gets a feel for people by taking their hands in his and letting his fingers read their attributes. He told me my exact height and weight after running his fingers across my palms for a few seconds.

Accept whatever you are granted.

ELLA MAY JONES
Age 68

*I*t used to be that I felt safe only when I was going through a hard time. You get accustomed to being miserable. The minute things got easier, I got nervous. I was sure the Lord was going to take it all away.

But a few years ago, I went to death's door. My heart attack was so bad, they had the morgue on the line when I came to. Now here I am, what they call a cardiac cripple. I can hardly move without getting short of breath. The strange thing is, I'm more peaceful than I've ever been.

I take each day one at a time. Whatever I can do, I do. Every day, I just bless the fact that I'm still here. Now, that's the way to live.

According to her daughter, Ella May Jones went from being a "nervous wreck" to living with Buddha-like calm after her heart attack. Her illness cordoned off manageable territory, which she presided over with confidence.

You never retire from the work of the spirit.

CHARLES ROBERTSON

Age 69

When I first retired, I was a lost soul. I would have gone right back to work if I hadn't gotten so sick. With all that time on my hands, I started wondering what I had made of my life. What was the point of it all? Did I accomplish anything worthwhile? I started picking everything apart.

If you stay with it, though, you start to figure things out. Maybe some of your mistakes weren't so bad after all. Maybe they were part of finding your way. Maybe you were heading somewhere all along, but didn't know it. Eventually, it hit me— Charlie, this is your work now. It's just a different kind of work, that's all, and there's plenty of it to do.

Shortly after Charles Robertson retired, a sequence of illnesses chipped away at his freedom. He was forced to give up driving, which meant that his range of activities shrank to what he could do at home. He became despondent to such a degree that his wife considered taking his shotgun out of the house. Once he identified his spiritual vocation, his range of inner activities became truly boundless.

I don't know how anyone can live without faith.

WALTER WAXMAN

Age 90

God's presence has been with me all of my life as a guide, as a comfort. I never disrespected people who didn't believe in God, I just felt sorry for them. I think it takes more effort to deny God than to sit back and accept Him. How else do you explain the beauty and order of nature?

Life is hard enough without trying to convince yourself that it's all one big chain of accidents. If I thought there was no rhyme or reason to life on earth, I wouldn't be able to bear it.

On a nonstop flight between New York and Munich, I sat next to *Walter Waxman, a missionary who was in the first leg of his journey back to India, and we debated aspects of faith—what it means to waver, how doubt can be vanquished, and what happens when faith cannot be attained at all. After about six animated hours, we were joined by one of the pilots who was taking a break in the passenger cabin. Soon all passengers within earshot were listening intently, but then a voice from several seats away interjected, "It's really good to have faith and all that, but who the hell is flying the plane?"*

It can take a lifetime to know why you are living.

GEORGE CALMENSON

Age 64

I used to be jealous of people who could say what they were living for, who had a purpose and could say what it was. I've done lots of different kinds of work, always followed my interests. I've been blessed with a lot of success, but in terms of goals, my life seemed haphazard. I liked how I was living, but couldn't explain it to myself or anyone.

Then, when I was sixty or so, I saw one clear thread running through everything I'd done. My purpose has been to follow my heart and accept that life leads me, not the other way around.

George Calmenson has changed careers the way some people change apartments, but his inner stance of goodness has been a constant large enough to be called a purpose. He now serves on the steering committee of a national organization seeking to return dignity and control to frail older people, no matter where they live, and this feels to him like a kind of culmination.

Marriage

You've got to have a little fire.

JERRY KLIMAN

Age 82

When I married Sara in 1942, I thought she was the most beautiful woman in the world. Every day of our life together, I have felt the same way.

People always wonder what makes a successful marriage. Well, I've been happily married for over fifty years and you've got me—though I think chemistry has a lot to do with it. I'm talking about good, old-fashioned passion. In my generation, people didn't wonder about these things, they just did them.

My wife is my best friend and lifelong companion. Every time I look at her, I still feel like the luckiest man around.

Jerry Kliman's grandson, Jed, looks at this photograph every day. He misses his grandfather a great deal, but what captivates him is the way his grandfather is looking at his grandmother. The look in his eyes isn't a young love remembered, but a present ardor undiminished by age.

One person can't give you everything.

HILDA HOFFMAN

Age 81

I've thought about this for years. The man who makes the best father to your children may not be the best husband, and vice versa. Father and husband require different qualities. My Joe was a first-rate father. The kids were crazy about him. But a husband? Dull as dull could be.

When the kids were all grown and gone, I thought I'd go nuts. Joe was loyal, reliable, clean, generous—how could I complain? But he had nothing to say, nothing I hadn't heard from him at least a hundred times already. When we went traveling, what saved me was the other people on the tour bus. Joe, he was asleep.

While raising their six children, Hilda Hoffman marveled at her husband's seemingly tireless patience. Instead of staying removed behind his newspaper, Joe got down on the floor and played with the kids. For years, she cherished her good fortune. But now she wonders what her life would have been like with another presumably more exciting kind of man.

Don't let any love affair keep you from your goals.

VIOLET BROWN

Age 92

My granddaughter says I'm a feminist. Well, I don't know about that, but I'll tell you I'm glad I've lived long enough to see women taking themselves seriously.

In my day, all we wanted was to find a man and devote our lives to him—to be swept off our feet. More often than not, we got swept into a corner. Everything we did was for our husbands, and we didn't question it. If we had any dreams of our own, we let them go, never to be seen again.

Take my life, for instance. We moved where my husband wanted to live. We traveled wherever he wanted to go. We did whatever he wanted to do. We even ate what he wanted to eat. Nowadays a woman doesn't have to put up with this.

Violet Brown was proud of the rights women had won in her lifetime. In her youth women were finally granted the right to vote. In her middle years, which included World War II, women began working some of the same jobs as men. In her later years women discovered that they could have their own lives. "It was too late for me," she said, "but it makes me so happy to see it."

There are many kinds of love.

LOUISE GARBER

Age 87

*M*y husband and I weren't much as lovers, but could we talk! His mind went in so many directions at once, I could hardly keep up with him. This was delightful. I was never bored in sixty years.

We had a fine life together. We came to an understanding. The details aren't anyone's business. People thought we were the ideal couple. No one could guess that the sparks didn't fly for us. Kindred spirits, yes, this they could see. And the love was there, a deep love. It was passionate, but just in a different way.

Today they would send us to counseling. They would tell us we put up with too much. Today passion is defined too nar-rowly, as sex. This is the silliest thing I've ever heard.

Louise Garber and her husband were known as a charismatic couple on the college campus where they taught. Once a week, they hosted salon-like gatherings for their students. Because others so obviously idealized their marriage and took hope from it, Louise and her husband didn't let on that an unusual compromise made their marriage work. Shortly before her death, Louise finally told the full story of their union to one of her former students.

Tension creates.

MAGGIE CORBIN
Age 92

on't be afraid to fight. Bring it on. Provoke each other. Get hot under the collar. It's good to have separate opinions. Arguments stir up passion. Differences are exciting. Show me a relationship without conflict and I'll show you boring.

While attending a friend's wedding shortly before my own, I was suddenly seized by doubt as I thought of all the unresolved conflicts that would soon be sealed in my own ceremony. I took refuge in the ladies' room, where Maggie Corbin, the bride's great-aunt, happened to be as well. "It's no problem," she assured me. "The best couples are the ones who get really mad and know how to have a good fight."

Marriage isn't easy.

MARTIN DEGEORGE

Age 99

hat makes a good marriage? Hard work. We should know. Harriet and I have been working at it for over seventy-five years. Young couples today think it's a piece of cake. Then, when it's rough, they give it up.

Sure, there have been times I wanted to walk out and never look back. Now I have to help her to the bathroom. You think that's fun? Half the time, we don't even get there in time. But she's still my sweet bride. We've had at least ten thousand misunderstandings, ten thousand hurts, and another ten thousand apologies.

Martin DeGeorge was just as frail as his wife, Harriet, yet he escorted her to the bathroom like she was a queen. Always the protective husband, he refused offers of household help, even though this meant he had to go on risking a steep flight of basement steps each time he did the laundry. "It would make her feel like less of a woman if I let a stranger in here," he whispered to me. "I'd rather sneak down there and get it all done myself than hurt Harriet's pride."

Blaming someone else is so much easier than looking at yourself.

EDEIN FRENCH

Age 84

When couples fight, most of the time neither person is listening. You're both putting all of your energy into arguing your own side. You're getting caught up in the enthusiasm of blaming, which is like a reflex. It requires no effort and happens automatically unless you oppose it with all your might.

But if one of you is able to stop and give the other some compassion, really try to see the other person's hurt, the steam goes right out of the fight. Something different happens, something interesting, instead of the same old fight again and again.

> *Edein French has been counseling couples for over fifty years. Nothing fazes her because she has seen every variety of conflict and reconciliation. Using her sharp mind and sensitive heart, she is relentless in teaching couples how to make their relationships work. At eighty-four, she still sees clients on an occasional basis, having chosen to slow down just a few years ago.*

You never know what goes on between two people.

JOSEPHINE DUNAWAY

Age 75

 am and I were together for almost fifty-two years, but no one could figure out what made us tick. We weren't the kind of couple that people considered meant for each other. Believe me, for a long time I couldn't understand it either.

In the beginning, it seemed like I was the one making all the compromises. I had to bend over backward to make things good for him. But when it was my turn to have it hard, Sam was there for me like you couldn't believe—a real rock. He paid me back many times over, and then some. From the outside looking in, this is the kind of thing you can't see.

At first glance, Sam and Josephine Dunaway did seem to be an unlikely match. He was volatile where she was serene. He hadn't read a book in fifty years, while she had a book in her hand at all times. He grumbled in bursts of rough-hewn or crude expressions, while she spoke with a measured, lilting cadence. But their devotion to one another was fervent.

Your marriage comes first, your children second.

SOPHIE GOLDFARB
Age 88

The two of you are the center of your family. Don't forget it. You are the ones who hold it all together. I see too many young couples today putting the kids first and each other second. That's a big mistake. Where are you supposed to get your strength? Sure, you get love from your kids, but don't think you won't end up lonely if you count on that in the long run.

Children don't want to be your only happiness. This puts too much pressure on them. When they see the two of you getting along, it gets them off the hook. It makes them feel more secure. Plus, they see the two of you having a good time together and it gives them hope, maybe someday they'll find somebody to be happy with. So don't let your marriage go down the drain because you're too busy catering to your kids.

Sophie Goldfarb's impassioned advice came directly from regret. She sadly described how the first flush of romance that had brought her and her husband, Wallace, together vanished shortly after they had children. When they occasionally managed to have time alone, they found their vat of conversation had been drained. Sophie now tries to warn every young couple she meets not to make these same mistakes.

Marriage isn't for everyone.

HARRY NICHOLS

Age 71

You start out with a lot of nice words. Then comes the hard part. You're supposed to compromise, but that wasn't for me. You're supposed to talk things over. I just waited for things to blow over. All six of my wives had the same complaints. I got sick of it. I'm better off single.

Living in wifeless freedom, Harry Nichols gradually became buried in the debris of daily living. His floors and furniture were covered with piles of tin cans and old newspaper, but he refused to accept the assistance of a county-funded housekeeper. In response to my pleas that he accept some help for the sake of his health and safety, he thundered, "I told you, I had enough of women messing around in my house."

Mutual respect—that's what enriches every day of married life.

FRANK WILLIAMS

Age 77

I am always learning from Carter, my wife. I respect her sensitivity to the people around her and her thoughtful approach to life. Occasionally, I don't handle something the way she prefers, but I want to hear what she has to say about it. That's how I've grown, for almost fifty years now. I think being interested in each other's point of view—whether or not you agree—is as important as taking pleasure in each other's company.

When asked to account for almost five decades of shared life, Frank Williams did not need to think it over. Mutual respect. *Indeed, he and his wife, Carter, emanate a powerful regard in each other's presence. Glancing at this photograph of Frank and Carter, a young man who was about to be married remarked, "I want a marriage like this."*

Being Blue

**Put your mind on something else,
or your troubles will take up
the whole world.**

HAZEL WOLF
Age 101

ou can't do two things at the same time. So if you're thinking about saving the environ‑ ment, you're not thinking about yourself and your problems. You can always find a way to be of service, in‑ stead of sitting home and watching TV. Help an organization do a mailing. Stuff envelopes. Get signatures on petitions. Make calls to get out the vote. There's always something use‑ ful you can do.

If you get out there and meet younger people naturally, you won't be alone when your friends and relatives start dying off. The generations are meant to be fluid, like a river, one running into another. All of these activities and the friendships that come with them keep you from feeling sorry for yourself and focusing on your aches and pains.

For more than forty years, Hazel Wolf was an active volunteer on be-half of social and environmental causes. She founded a local branch of the Audubon Society, and frequently gave speeches at marches and demonstrations. On the afternoon she died, she was busy putting the finishing touches on an environmental newsletter she edited. She gave to her community until the last moments of her life.

Kids don't care if you're old, only if you're fun.

MARIA SANCHEZ
Age 80

When I get to feeling blue, my neighbor boy Billy is the best company there is. He's five. We sit out on the curb and play with the ants. We don't kill them, we just give them a little trouble getting back to their nest. We pile up twigs, or put a big shoe in the way.

Billy always knows how I'm feeling, without my saying a word. He doesn't notice I'm an old lady, except for when it's time to get me back on my feet. Then it's a real production. First, I have to roll over onto the grass. Once I get myself onto my hands and knees, he helps me haul myself up the rest of the way. I moan and groan and put on a good show. He thinks it's great. By that time, I'm usually feeling pretty great, too.

Maria Sanchez lived in a low-income housing community where older adults resided alongside younger adults with disabilities, and families with small children. When she first moved there, she was afraid that the noise and activity of the children would be too much for her. But over time, as her friendship with Billy grew, she noticed that her arthritis pained her the least on the days she spent a lot of time with him.

Cherish your old friends—you won't always have them.

BETTY BROWN
Age 89

The world feels emptier since Gertrude died. We were best friends since kindergarten, and we'd talk every week. Now when the phone rings Sunday morning, I still jump up, thinking, "That's Gertrude." I know I'll always feel blue on Sundays, missing her.

You shouldn't ever pass up a chance to spend time with an old friend. Sure, plane tickets are expensive. Maybe you don't like her husband. Even if you don't see things eye to eye any more—what's the difference? An old friend can tease you like no one else can. She's got the goods on you. She knew your parents. She was with you before either of you knew who you were. There's all the old stories, all the old laughs. After you lose her, there's no getting any of that back.

Betty Brown's daughter begged her to go to a senior center. "Mom, you have to make new friends," she implored. But Betty remained firm, stating, "I could make forty new friends, but no one can take Gertrude's place."

Doing good gets you out of bed in the morning.

GRACE STANCHFIELD

Age 96

My daughter-in-law Erla's favorite phrase was, "Be kind to each other." In the months right after she died, I fell into a funk. I didn't want to get out of bed in the morning, and I began spending the afternoons sleeping. One morning I woke up with her words on my mind. I asked myself, what kindness can I give to the people here? This retirement home is such a lonely place, there must be something I can do for someone.

Ever since, I've been finding out how right Erla was. The smallest things can make a big difference, like holding a heavy door for someone, or noticing what a pretty dress someone is wearing. You can see good cheer go right into some of the sour faces and maybe bring a smile. I get out of bed now with quite a bit to do, and the blues are gone.

While severe macular degeneration has taken away most of Grace Stanchfield's sight, she continues to bless the community around her with her generosity. She also participates in a study of the aging brain, frequently taking the bus to the research center where she undergoes batteries of tests. It gives her great satisfaction to know that her brain will be analyzed in detail after she dies, as an example of someone maintaining mental acuity long into her nineties.

Getting older, you have to get tougher.

ALTHEIA ANDERSON
Age 88

eople my age are dropping like flies. Everywhere I go, it seems I'm the oldest one there. You start to feel like you're the only one left, like your whole generation is going. That's because it is. I have to make myself read the obituaries every day just to keep up. Otherwise, I'd send out my Christmas cards and get half of them back marked "deceased." That's the worst way to find out.

I'm trying to get a thicker skin. "Don't be going to no pity party," I tell myself, "or that's all you'll be doing."

Altheia Anderson talked tough but had soft eyes and a tender manner. She was active on the residents' council of her senior apartment complex, but she grew weary of the constant turnover from people dying. As newcomers joined the council, Altheia found herself resistant to getting attached to them. "I've got to push myself to keep the door open," she told me, as she delivered a basket of brownies to a resident who had just moved in.

It's nobody's business how you do your grieving.

HENRIETTA SAMUELS

Age 91

Ever since Ralph died, I've been going into our big closet in the bedroom and sniffing his clothes. I squeeze myself in there, right between his suits. That's where his smell is the strongest. Especially when I'm feeling blue, I go in there and get a good, long sniff. It's the only place in the house where it doesn't feel like he's gone.

One afternoon, my daughter came over while I was still in that closet, sniffing. I guess I didn't hear the bell. She used her key, and the next thing I knew I heard her calling me in the hall. I tried to sneak out of the closet, but some hangers gave me away. She asked what the heck I was doing in there. I thought she was going to have me locked up. She threatened to throw all of his clothes in her car that minute and donate them to charity. I let her know that closet was going to stay just the way it was.

Henrietta Samuels' husband, Ralph, was a salesman who spent most of his working years on the road. Because he moved his family each time his territory was shifted, Henrietta barely had time to accumulate acquaintances before they were packing up to leave. She became adept at departures and absences, fleeting relationships, and making do with whatever warmth she could find.

You are the master of your mind.

ART SORNBERGER

Age 90

When you're feeling badly, you can tell your mind to focus on something else. Your mind is not your master. You can control how you think and exactly what you think about. It takes effort, but this is something you can learn how to do. It gets easier with practice.

This gives you power over your own life. The way you think about things greatly affects how you feel and therefore how you live.

When Art Sornberger is asked his opinion on a matter of significance, he often defers any commentary until he has had sufficient time to ponder. Then people lean forward to hear his raspy, barely audible voice, knowing his remarks will be worth the wait.

Don't keep your tears to yourself.

GEORGE ESTABON

Age 79

*I*t wasn't till my stroke that anyone ever saw me cry. Even when Ethel died, I didn't shed a tear—after fifty-two years of marriage. I was too proud. That's how I was brought up. Stiff upper lip. Keep your feelings to yourself. Pull yourself up by your bootstraps. Ethel always said, "George, you hold too much in."

Well, I never did let anything out, not while I still had her, anyway. I just couldn't do it. But five years later, my stroke did it. The part of my brain that controls emotions got damaged, and there I was, half paralyzed, blubbering like a baby. I think I must have cried seventy years' worth of tears all at once.

As terrible as it was, the relief was tremendous. My daughter says I'm acting like the father she always wanted. Can you believe it? I'm emotional. If there's a spirit world, I know Ethel's impressed.

George Estabon made use of his damaged brain as the vehicle of his liberation. Where many men withdraw from relationships in order to control the flow of their feelings, George allowed his loss of inhibitions to usher him into a new phase of life.

Whatever happens, don't cave in.

JOHN LESTER
Age 82

*G*etting old requires *chutzpah*. You can't just sit around, hoping good things will come to you. If you do, you'll only fall through the cracks into deep disappointment. I see too many old people giving up, going limp, waiting for the rabbi to come bury them.

I was afraid of computers, but I wanted to write a book. I could have pounded it out on my old manual typewriter, or—better yet—stayed with my trusty pencil. Instead, I took the plunge with an obsolete piece of machinery someone was throwing away. I did it. I learned how to write on a computer. Now I have a manuscript over three hundred pages long and still multiplying.

Let's face it. The rabbi will come soon enough. In the meantime, you have to go out there and make sure you get what you need. You have to make things happen.

When he turned eighty, John Lester began an experiment with memory. He wanted to recall boyhood details of the prewar Jewish East End of London, a time when that section of the city still resembled the Eastern European origins of its inhabitants. Day after day, he sat in his apartment, beckoning back images of this vanished world. He jotted down the inventive pranks of his gang of rascal friends, glimpses of bagel makers standing on street corners, and the enchanting smells of his neighborhood as mothers prepared for the Sabbath meal.

Work

The best things in life aren't always the easiest.

OLE HATLEN

Age 96

Being young is tricky. You have to figure out what to do with your life. That's really hard. Playing the piano was what I loved. I practiced for hours on end while other children ran around playing games. No one had to force me to sit down at the piano. That's what I wanted to do.

When I grew up, it was the same way. Everyone told me it would be easier to earn a living doing something else. They said just about *anything* else would be easier. I'm sure this is true. But I did what I loved.

Severely affected by Alzheimer's disease, Ole Hatlen generally doesn't remember his career as a concert pianist. Occasionally, he has bursts of clarity when his early life breaks through. Once, I asked him to play something on the piano for me. He insisted that he didn't know how. Assuring him that hands have a memory all their own, I helped him onto a piano bench and placed his hands on the keys. He began fingering the keys soundlessly, but then suddenly his hands dove into an étude by Chopin, thundering over the keyboard with virtuoso skill. Ole was amazed, a spectator to his own resurgence.

Getting what you want takes hard work.

ED MARKSMAN

Age 71

For a long time, I tried everything under the sun, except working hard. I was sure I would be the guy to outsmart the system, to get something for nothing.

I found out that nothing is what you get for nothing. After a while, I started asking people how they got to where they were. "Hard work." That's what each one said, one after the other. "Hard work." It was like a broken record, but I had to hear it at least a hundred times before I thought it applied to me. That's the thing of it—you usually don't listen to the ones who really know.

Ed Marksman was determined that I heed his advice, repeating it every time I saw him. Each rendition included new flourishes of self-flagellation designed to lend his words credence and the impact they deserved. He hoped to make some use of his hard-won experience by making a difference in someone else's life.

If you earn a living one way, that doesn't mean that's all you do with your life.

IRWIN LUSTBADER

Age 72

These days, there's so much pressure to specialize. Everybody thinks he has to find a niche and stay there. That's a lot of foolishness. Don't box yourself in or narrow yourself down. Develop as many parts of yourself as you can. Follow your yearnings. You might earn a living from one of your interests, but you can still explore others.

One interest feeds another. Our minds are not compartmentalized, so why should our lives be like that?

My father, Irwin Lustbader, always encouraged me to develop many interests at the same time. He spent thirty years as a junior high school social studies teacher, bemoaning with a smile that 10 percent of his time was spent teaching and the other 90 percent dealing with the chaos caused by surging adolescent hormones. During summer breaks, he would follow his fascination with Native American culture by donning a feathered headdress and teaching Indian lore from inside a teepee at various day camps.

Make sure your ambitions lead to the kind of life you want to live.

JOHN COOPER

Age 72

I was always dissatisfied with my job, thinking it must be better for the guys on top. I didn't know that 90 percent of all jobs is scut work, no matter how high or low your position. Even the guy making a million dollars a year has lots of trash to take care of. But I had no idea this was so, and I gave up a lot, clawing my way to high places.

Finally, years and years later, after there wasn't any higher to go, I saw the lay of the land. It's the same for the CEO as the mail clerk. It's smarter to seek out work you really like and stay there than to chase after achievement that might be nothing special once you get there.

As CEO of a large corporation, John Cooper had attained everything he ever wanted professionally—wealth, power, and position. The cost was eighteen-hour days. Retiring meant he had been released from his ambitions at last. He had hoped to make up for lost time with his two daughters and his son, but by this time they were too busy with families and careers of their own. "I feel like I missed their childhoods," he said, noticing how rarely he was present in family photographs.

If you're always behind, you never really get anywhere.

MURRAY MARTIN

Age 75

You can spend your whole life putting things off. I didn't face up to this until I was an old man. Can you imagine? I waited till I was in my seventies. At work, I was famous for getting to meetings at least a half hour late and turning in my paperwork after it had started turning yellow. The bosses put up with me, but I never did get promoted.

Work is work, whether you get it done now, next week, or next month. The job still has to be done, so you might as well do it now. If you're smart, you'll get it done early and it will be off your back that much sooner.

You know what cured me? Last year, my best friend was in the hospital. Did I go visit him? No, I put it off. Then he died. Before I got there, he was gone. That was it. I had enough with procrastination. Now whenever I go somewhere, I get there early. I take the bus *before* the last bus. I never wait until the last minute with anything. I take care of business, one, two, three. I can hardly believe this is me. I would have gone far in life if I had figured this out sooner.

Murray Martin expelled procrastination from his life in one decisive swipe, but it happened too late to transform his work life into something he could be proud of. By giving this speech every chance he gets, he takes great pleasure in trying to cure others who procrastinate.

Your true work may be waiting for you.

JOHN SCOTT

Age 73

When I was twenty years old, I was on a ship that was sunk by a German sub. We drifted in a lifeboat in the middle of the Pacific Ocean for more than two months. Our provisions ran out in wthree weeks. We caught every drop of rainwater, but the hunger we experienced was nothing compared to the thirst.

I decided to accept what each day brought, rather than struggle against it. I concentrated on the sky—the colors, the shapes, the different kinds of light. The other guys laughed at me, but I ignored them. Then they thought I was praying. One by one, the men who couldn't get their minds off their thirst died.

From then on, long after the war, I saw colors and shapes and light all the time, paintings in my mind, but I didn't actually paint until I was sixty. When I finally picked up a brush and started painting, I realized that this was my true work. If only I had listened to myself the way I did on that lifeboat! Now I'm in a rush when I could have had a lifetime as an artist.

John Scott took up painting in his sixties and completed more than fifty canvases. Then he challenged himself with photography. He photographed raindrops on flowers, clouds surging and receding, distortions of buildings reflected by neighboring windows, and glimpses of people pausing in urban pursuits. Every month, he set aside a portion of his meager Social Security check in order to develop a rationed number of rolls of film. He was a Buddhist who believed in striving for deep receptivity in experiencing life, yet he also believed in accepting impermanence. Shortly before he died, John gave a few paintings to friends and asked that the rest be donated to a local art school so that students in need could reuse his canvases.

Retirement is a ridiculous idea.

BEN RAIL

Age 92

I've retired three or four times already. Sitting in a rocking chair is boring. When you work, you meet lots of people. It keeps your mind off things. Otherwise you get stuck in a rut and stay there.

I rode rodeo for five years, had my own welding business, even ran a doughnut shop until the war came and they started rationing oil and sugar. I've dabbled a little in just about everything. I'd always had a hankering to get my hands into some clay, but I didn't get a chance till now. I turned eighty-nine and opened up a ceramics studio.

Lots of people come to my shop, work on their projects, and have a good time. Meanwhile, I'm making a few dollars, and my supplies are all paid for. You can't beat that. I just don't believe in retirement.

Greeting visitors to his ceramics shop, Ben Rail doesn't dash off a shop-keeper's ready-to-serve welcome, but rather seems truly glad for the chance to meet yet another of life's wayfarers. The time he spends with his customers makes them eager to return, as much to be in his company as to paint a sumptuous glaze on a salad bowl.

Illness and Frailty

If you accept help, you teach the next generation how to give help.

DOROTHY BOBROW

Age 86

My mother was pushing ninety, but she still wouldn't let us give her a hand with anything. "I'm fine." That's all she'd say, but we knew she wasn't. She had heart problems, breathing problems, you name it, just like I do now. And look at me! I've been pushing everyone away, just like she did. It's my pride. I don't want to have to depend on anyone. I want to stand on my own two feet. But it's hard for me to carry my laundry basket and use my cane at the same time. The other day, I let my granddaughter do a wash for me. You should have seen her face, so proud to be helping her grandma. I know this is the way it should be.

Dorothy Bobrow, my grandmother, spent her childhood on New York City's Lower East Side. She was the eleventh and youngest child of immigrant parents, one of seven sisters who kept in close contact throughout their adult lives. The sisters were perplexed by their mother's refusal to depend on any of them in her old age. It was not until my grandmother was also in her eighties that she began to understand her mother's attitude.

Give people a break when they're in pain.

SADIE FARBER
Age 88

I never wanted to be like this. I growl at everyone who tries to help me. It's awful. The nicer someone is to me, the nastier I am. There isn't a bone in my body that doesn't bother me, night and day.

I wish somebody would say, "Hey, I don't blame you. I'd be irritable, too." That would take a load off my shoulders. I can't even unscrew a bottle of ketchup myself. I have to grit my teeth and say "please" and "thank you." I just don't qualify to be Saint Sadie.

Despite her tendency to snarl, Sadie Farber was beloved to the home health aides who assisted her. She had a way of lacing her nastiness with wit, and no one left her house without having had a good laugh or two. She had tiny fractures throughout her spine and legs due to bone loss, a condition for which there is no remedy once it occurs and which is quite painful.

Being interested—that's what makes life interesting.

TOM SULLIVAN

Age 78

There's an awful lot you can learn watching people. Looking out my window, sitting down in the lobby—there's plenty to see. Everybody asks me, "Aren't you restless?" Sure, I can't go anywhere anymore. Big deal. I'm tethered to an oxygen tank, but what am I missing? All those nurses come to see me. It's a regular parade. Each one's got a story. Each one tells me what to do, what not to do, what to eat, what not to eat. Do this, don't do that. I humor them. I make them feel good. Nobody ever needs to be bored, even when you're sicker than a dog and stuck at home all the time.

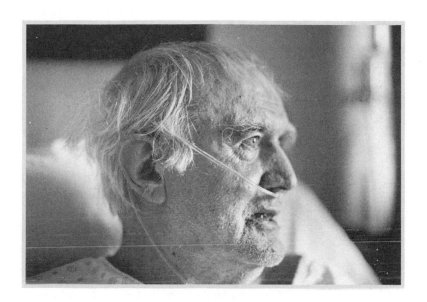

Tom Sullivan was homebound for most of the last decade of his life, too frail to venture out of his apartment in a shabby old hotel. When nurses came to listen to his lungs, he always preferred hearing something about his visitors' lives to talking about his physical travails. Once he became fond of a particular nurse, he would decorate a paper plate with a star and the nurse's name, then tape it to the wall. As his life filled with the nurses' affection, his wall gradually filled with stars.

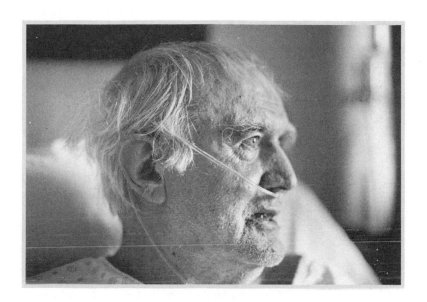

Nobody wants to be somebody else's burden.

TILLIE BECKER
Age 83

Back home, I had friends galore. I had my card games. I had places to walk. It was a life. But then, it seemed like moving near my daughter was the sensible thing to do. You know—blood is thicker than water. I was turning eighty, getting to where I might need some help, so I figured it was time.

But I should have known. Kids have their own lives. Busy, busy, busy. It's a big deal when they're able to fit in a little time for me. I feel like I'm just one more task on each of their lists. I can see it in their eyes—coming over here is an obligation, not a pleasure. My grandson carries around a little computer that tells him when he can see his grandma and for how long. Everybody's always looking at the clock.

You know what you wish for at my age? That you have people around who enjoy you. My friends and I loved being together. I had it good with them. I wish I'd stayed put.

Tillie Becker saw the approach of potential frailty and tried to be prudent. She told me that she made her decision to move near her family after one of her friends had fallen and broken her hip. Her friend had a great deal of difficulty finding paid helpers to assist her after her return from the hospital, and then one of these helpers stole some valuable items from her apartment while she was taking a nap. That was it for Tillie—she put her condo up for sale.

You're brought down so low, your worries don't matter anymore.

EVELYN GROSSKOPF

Age 78

When you get sick, you have to accept things you never thought you'd accept. You can't do things your own way anymore. It's always the way other people want to do things, because you're the one that needs their help. You have to wait for this, wait for that. Everybody knows your business. Your pride? Forget it.

But a lot of things get easier after you hit bottom. What have you got to lose? You already lost it. You don't even know why it used to be such a big deal to make your bed a certain way or to fold the linen so neatly or keep the floor so clean. Your worries seem like they were from another lifetime.

For most of her life, Evelyn Grosskopf found asking for help unthink-able. Her fierce dignity had helped her survive the Holocaust and many hardships thereafter. Even with her strength waning from cancer, she spent many mornings crawling on her hands and knees around her white-tiled apartment, scrubbing each tile individually with a cloth be-cause she could no longer handle a mop.

Dying isn't so terrible—it's what precedes it that's frightening.

RUDY CLARK

Age 76

What if one day I can't get to the bathroom on my own? What if I can't swallow right and they have to give me ground-up mush? What if they have to cart me here and there, like a sack of potatoes? What if I turn into one of those mixed-up ones that doesn't know if he's coming or going? What if this, what if that? It seems that everyone I know is afraid of these "what ifs" more than they're afraid of dying.

I think it's time we figured out better ways to handle these situations. I'd like to see a whole group of doctors doing nothing but this—making sure people aren't stuck up the creek without a paddle. Dying seems pretty simple by comparison.

Those who carry peaceful images of their parents' last days often derive hope and comfort from these memories. Having seen his own mother die a lonely death, Rudy Clark found it hard to believe that the time before dying could go well. I assured him that some people are able to depend on others, to find out that they are loved and that they can count on others' loyalty. He brushed this aside, insisting on bleak possibilities.

A knock at the door can mean so much.

SUE POWERS
Age 87

I remember how I thought of old ladies like me years ago—they were *cute*. In my family, there were lots of great-aunts, shrunken and shriveled ladies living by themselves in tiny apartments, neat as a pin, with pretty teacups. They were so happy to see me when I bothered to drop by on my way somewhere else. That's how it was. I gave them the crumbs of my life, five minutes here and there. It never occurred to me that they were once just like me, that I could pull up a chair and get to know them as people, not just porcelain dolls.

Now I'm a shrunken old lady stuck in my apartment, and I know how those aunts of mine waited and hoped and waited for a visitor to brighten their day. My nieces do come over, but it's once in a blue moon. I never know when. A visitor is like gold. It's too bad we can't understand this when we're young and can still do something about it.

166

Sue Powers couldn't leave her second-floor apartment because she had a terror of elevators, and her lungs were unable to bear the exertion of stairs. She paid people in the building two dollars to get her a quart of milk and a loaf of bread at the convenience store across the street. The income from her Social Security check barely took care of her necessities, but she regarded her lack of visitors as her true poverty.

Treat people in wheelchairs just like anyone else.

JAKE NELSON

Age 68

It makes my skin crawl when someone says I'm brave. "Oh, you're so courageous, living with multiple sclerosis for so many years." What else am I supposed to do? There's nothing brave about it. These are the cards I've been dealt. I have to bear my fate just like anybody else. I didn't choose it. I don't like being in a wheelchair. People stare at you or they look away as fast as they can. I wish people would understand—we're not any different. We're just making do with what we've got.

Jake Nelson hates calling attention to his disability, but he goes wild when able-bodied people stand in curb cuts and he can't cross the street without first making a commotion: "You have to yell to get their attention, point to where they're standing, and wait for them to figure it out. By then, the light has changed."

Don't fight things you can't change.

SOPHIE NOBLE

Age 86

or a long time after I lost my sight, I was going to doctors, looking for them to make things better for me. I felt cheated. Why did this have to happen to me? I can't even read the directions on the back of a frozen meal.

Just recently, something in me clicked. I woke up one morning and said to myself, "I want to live, so this is it." I have certain medical problems, and they're not going to get any better. It's time to start living again—a different life, but at least it's life. Now I wake up in the morning and I'm not complaining. My son writes the directions with a thick marker on the back of my frozen meals.

Having lost most of her vision, Sophie Noble uprooted herself from a community where she had resided for over fifty years. She did not want to burden her friends with looking after her, and so moved three thousand miles away to a son and daughter-in-law's community. There, despite her family's ample tenderness and solicitude, she fell into a period of mourning the loves and liberties she had lost.

Good Conduct

After a certain age, we make our lives what they are.

PAT GREEN
Age 97

The most fortunate people are the ones who have been taught how to act right. From an early age, they learned the basics—what's good and bad, what's true and false.

If your upbringing left these things blurry, life can get messy in a hurry. People who are unhappy in their lives get into trouble, and then they end up losing respect for themselves. Once they lose their self-respect, they get even more unhappy and get into more trouble. It becomes a sad, awful circle.

There's only one way out of the mess—plain decency. You can always start to honor yourself by how well you act. At some point in your life, you either go on heaping shame upon yourself or you start doing things in a way that makes you proud. It's your choice.

Pat Green's father was a church deacon. One year the minister ran off with one of the choir girls, a friend of Pat's sixteen-year-old sister. From that day on, Pat's father never again went to church, and that was the end of any instruction on faith for Pat. She had, however, been taught by this episode something essential about the conduct of one's life.

Before you blurt out your feelings, consider where you're heading.

HERB JOHNSON
Age 86

People generally let themselves be driven by emotion. They speak before they give themselves a chance to think about what they want to say. They often end up regretting what comes out of their mouths.

A long time ago, I taught myself to stop and think before I said anything. I still always pause and ask myself, "What do I really want to achieve?" Usually, what I'm about to say in the heat of the moment isn't going to get me any closer to where I want to go, so I don't say it. If you keep your eye on the target, you don't get into trouble.

A flair for getting along with people has furthered Herb Johnson's life for almost all of his eighty-six years. He rose through the ranks of a large company, earning respect by forging alliances and giving assistance across departmental lines. Now he uses his ample skills while serving on community boards, gliding past petty tensions, and cajoling others into uncommon levels of cooperation.

Make a habit of honesty.

MINNIE NIGHTHAWK
Age 87

When I was a girl, my father taught me how to hunt, saying a woman should know how to take care of herself. My dear mother taught me two lessons—to eat breakfast in the morning, and to make honesty a way of life. Both should happen every day, she said, not become things you choose to do now and then.

Dishonest situations give you a lot of stress in life. Think about how hard it is to remember when and where you lied about something, and what exactly you said. It gives you a headache.

I've had very little stress because I learned so early to tell the truth. I haven't had to worry about keeping things straight. This is why I have so few wrinkles.

When I came upon Minnie Nighthawk sitting on a park bench, I saw a woman of striking radiance who looked both young and old. Around her neck was intricate beadwork, and matching earrings were draped alongside her smooth cheeks. When I told her I was trying to learn from older people what makes a good life, she remarked, "You're asking the right person the right question."

Don't keep secrets, or you'll be lonely.

ETHEL HUNTINGTON
Age 91

I didn't tell anyone, not my brothers, not my mother, not my husband, not my closest girlfriends. I still haven't told my children. I was too ashamed and didn't want them to think badly of my father's memory.

It's done me damage, though, keeping it all inside. I never got close to anyone when I could have. I was afraid people could see right into me, so I always kept a certain distance. I ended up building my life around my secret, without realizing it.

Now I see it. If you hide part of yourself, no one ever really knows you. You pay a high price if you let shame fence you in.

Ethel Huntington confessed her most dire secret to me after she heard the term "sexual abuse" on Oprah's television show. "I didn't know they had a name for it," she told me, "but it happened to me." Several weeks went by before she was able to tell me that her father was the one who did that to her. She was proud of herself for breaking out of her self-imposed isolation at long last.

When in doubt, try the truth.

MARTHA EASTMAN
Age 80

I've always been a bit of a pushover. All you ever heard from me was "I don't know" or "That's fine." I didn't even know what it was I thought. My husband, Leo, was the one with the opinions.

After Leo died, my girlfriend dragged me to a current events class at the senior center, just to get me out of the house. The teacher went around and asked each person's opinion about a war somewhere. I opened my mouth and out came some ideas, *my* ideas. It was the strangest thing—to speak my mind, to hear what was on my mind, to know I even had a mind of my own.

I haven't stopped spouting since. If you don't know how to do it, just reach inside yourself and call it the way you see it. There's nothing quite like it. Truth has a ring to it. People know it when they hear it, even when it's something they don't want to hear. It startles them. It wasn't until I got to be an old lady that I found this out, and now you can't shut me up.

Overturning more than sixty years of timidity and accommodation was like a revelation to Martha Eastman. Her husband had been so dominant and uncompromising that her own point of view gradually receded somewhere deep inside. It was only during her widowhood that she began to heed the stirrings of her own truth.

Be yourself.

CHARLOTTE PASSIKOFF

Age 84

I've been myself all my life, but that's gotten me into a lot of trouble. I've told teachers what I think. I've told bosses how I feel. I've been straightforward, even when it cost me a good grade in school or a promotion on the job. My mother used to be shocked at how I was. She'd look at me, shaking her head, saying in Yiddish, *"Was ist drinnin Ling ist offen Zing,"* "What's in your heart is on your tongue." It sounds better in Yiddish, but you get the idea.

Don't get me wrong. I'm a caring person. I tried not to hurt other people. When I worked, I didn't kiss up to anyone above me or step on anyone beneath me. I just couldn't hide the way I felt, and after a while I didn't try.

You should live the way you think is right. Don't concern yourself with other people's opinions. Never put on airs. Don't try to be somebody you're not.

Charlotte Passikoff's father disciplined her and her sister with lectures more severe than any kind of hitting. Almost eighty years later, she still insists, "Sometimes it would have been easier to get a whack across the can than to endure one of those talks." Charlotte is not sure how her father developed his strong character, but she is sure of the origin of hers.

Treat your one and only body with respect.

HARRIET SULLIVAN

Age 67

*L*isten to me. Do something about your bad habits when you're young. Other-wise, you'll be sorry later. It's so easy to trick yourself. You say, "I'll deal with it later," or, "Tomorrow I'll clean up my act." It sounds really good, doesn't it? But it's a lie. It's just buying time to keep on doing what you're doing.

Now I'm chained to an oxygen tank. I regret every cigarette I ever smoked. I made those same excuses every day. "It calms me down." "It helps me concentrate." What bunk! You don't get a second chance. I'd scream it from the rooftops, if I had enough air.

Harriet Sullivan was a chain smoker for over forty years while sitting in bars and drinking away her self-respect. At age sixty, she gave up both cigarettes and alcohol in one determined leap, but her lungs had already been ruined. Her spirit made a recovery so inspiring to others that she became the centerpiece of my clinic's group for people trying to achieve sobriety. I watched in awe as younger alcoholics facing Harriet's fiery candor were propelled out of self-destruction.

You can have as many children as you want.

EMMA BRADDOCK
Age 69

They took out my uterus before I turned twenty-one. Cancer. I went around feeling sorry for myself. My friends were all having babies, popping them out one, two, three, while I pined away. *Barren.* What an awful word.

Well, it got to the point where things had to go one way or another—either live my life as a desert, or be fruitful and multiply, just in a different way. I ended up raising one stepson and helping out about fifteen other kids along the way. There's no lack of kids needing to be loved. Just look around. Last year, when I had my heart attack, every last one of my kids came to my door. "Emma, let me get you some groceries. Emma, can't I vacuum your living room?" They were falling over each other trying to do things for me.

There was standing room only in the bedroom where Emma Braddock lived her last days. She would open her eyes for just a few minutes every afternoon, but each time, she saw devotion in the faces surrounding her bed.

Eat, and do right.

ETHEL JONES
Age 99

I was born in 1901. I got to Seattle in 1942. In those days, people didn't even know how to dress downtown. It's so different now. It seems buildings go up overnight.

It's hard for me to get around. My legs get so tired. Crossing the street, I'm only halfway across when those cars are ready to run me over. I make my way as fast as I can and that's the best I can do. My feet swell up something awful, but they go down at night. I don't take any medicine. I only go to the doctor when I absolutely have to.

If you want to live a long time, keep your mind on the simple things. Don't make things too complicated.

I struck up a conversation with Ethel Jones at a bus stop. She had a lively face, and her spirit turned out to be as spunky as her countenance. Our conversation accelerated from small talk to wisdom about life in just a few minutes. As my bus approached and I bade her good-bye, she called after me, "Be sure to eat, and do right."

You have to be able to say you're sorry.

NELLIE NICKERSON
Age 81

 lot of people can't say "I'm sorry" at all, and some say it too easily. If you're going to say it, you should mean it. A person has to sit down and analyze herself, "Was I really wrong?" and then admit it. This is something I've always tried to do.

The other half of apologizing is being able to accept someone else's apology. But when someone wrongs me, I don't forgive easily. Believe me, I'm not bragging. If someone really hurts me, I'd rather never see that person again. This isn't good.

Nellie Nickerson has a generous, welcoming spirit that has made her beloved to a host of friends and family members. Her sense of humor is always there to rescue a moment of awkwardness or dislodge someone's irritation. But she sees herself maintaining a major flaw in the conduct of her relationships and, in her eighth decade, is still trying to correct this.

The answers are there in your own heart.

NEDRA EDMONDS
Age 91

When you're not sure about something, stop and ask yourself: Is it true? Is it right? See what comes to you. You'll know what to do. You really have to stop and listen to yourself. Not everyone does. You get better at this as you have more life experience. You reach the point where you can trust in what you know. But it helps to have lived a long time.

Nedra Edmonds often asks where she is supposed to be and what she is supposed to be doing. Alzheimer's disease has afflicted her with the anxiety of being unable to get her bearings. But because of her innate good nature, when she is engaged in talking with a group of people, she takes an interest in them and flourishes in the warmth of their company. Sometimes she breaks into song.

On

Regret

Everyone misses out on something.

PAUL STIER

Age 91

Some things affect you your whole life, like growing up without a mother's love. My mother left me and my brother when we were young. I still don't know why. My brother was just two, so he didn't remember her at all. I was five.

Our dad was good to us. What can I say? He did his best. He put food on the table. I'm not knocking him at all. I just always wondered what it would have been like to have had a mother.

A father is not a mother. When other boys would complain about their mothers, I wanted to pop them one and tell them to shut up. Be grateful you *have* a mother!

Paul Stier's gruff and silent father never told him why his mother left the family when he was a young boy. Paul became a carpet salesman and married a loving and spirited woman with whom he enjoyed more than sixty years of marriage. He had one daughter. The year before he died, his granddaughter brought him a two-day-old great-granddaughter to hold in his arms.

If you really want to do something, don't let yourself off the hook.

MATILDA JOHANSEN
Age 101

ere I am, an old woman already. I always thought I had a book inside me. Every year I told myself, "Next year you'll write your book." The years came and went. It always seemed like next year I'd start in on it, but I never did—and I've had a whole century.

If you have a book inside you, sit down and get it written. It's not a matter of having the time. If you want to do something badly enough, you do it. You set other things aside and you make it a priority. You stop giving your life away to obligations.

Now my hands are twisted up with arthritis and I can't see beyond the end of my nose. See? I have the time, but now I can't do it.

Matilda Johansen had one great satisfaction before she died: she got to see her remorse turn into another person's inspiration. When I met Matilda, I had a book on my mind that wasn't getting written, and the usual host of excuses. Matilda's story of her own unwritten book ran through me like an electric current. From then on, she asked me each week what progress I'd made, and I never disappointed her.

Beware of your prejudices—the life you condemn may be your own.

JIM WENTWORTH
Age 68

I spent too much of my life as a snob. My specialty was behind-the-back ridicule. No one escaped my harsh tongue, but I particularly despised people on welfare, people who sat back and let the government take care of them.

Then when my heart attack did me in, I was only fifty-eight. I had to quit work. My savings went in a flash, and my disability check didn't even cover my mortgage. I landed in a subsidized apartment. My first few days, I wouldn't even go down to get my mail. I couldn't stand being one of *them.*

One morning there was a knock at my door. One of my neighbors handed me a pie and welcomed me to the building. Later, another asked me if I needed anything at the store. It's been almost ten years now. I've made the best friends I've ever had. My door is always open. People seek me out for advice, a shoulder to cry on, you name it. I wish I had spent my life like this. I'm making up for lots of lost time.

People still talk about Jim Wentworth at the public housing project where he spent his last days. Once he discovered the power of kindness, first by receiving it and then by giving it many times over, he missed no opportunities. Shortly before he died, he told me, "Nothing I attained as a successful businessman comes close to what I've gained here, in my supposed poverty."

Learn how to speak up for yourself.

HIROKO TOMITA
Age 82

I kept quiet most of my life. I was taught as a child not to make trouble, not to complain, not to burden my parents. If something bad was going on, I didn't say a word. I was good. I endured. But things are different these days. I listen to talk shows on the radio. Everyone complains! I think this is better. Why should you keep quiet? You should learn how to speak up for yourself. Otherwise, the ones who cause trouble get their way and the good ones pay the price. I know it's hard to change in your eighties, but I am trying.

Hiroko Tomita tries to time her visits to Mount Rainier to coincide with the brief blooming of the wildflowers. Trudging up steep walkways above the lodge, she manages to reach vantage points that few people in their eighties ever see. She walks with a slow, determined diligence that leaves no doubt she will get there, in her own way and in her own time.

The vessel that carries your spirit is fragile.

SHELBY JOHNSON
Age 83

When I retired, I bought a waterfront house with steep steps leading up to the garage. I thought I was exempt—old age was never going to happen to me. What hubris!

It's easy to take your strength for granted. Until it happens, you can't imagine being done in by a flight of steps. But when you're old, all it takes is a bad spell of the flu and—bingo—your legs are like noodles.

You see? It's better to face it. The human body is vulnerable, pure and simple. I wish I had accepted this and acted accordingly. Instead, look at me now—trapped. Don't let this happen to you.

Shelby Johnson's magnificent water view was the envy of all who visited his house, until he could no longer get to his garage. Then his house robbed him of his freedom and independence. Once, in my early forties, I told a realtor, "Don't bother showing me any houses with steep steps, no matter how lovely the view." She looked at me uncomprehendingly—probably because she was thirty-three.

Say what you have to say, before it's too late.

MILDRED POTTER

Age 77

I always wanted to tell my dad how much it meant to me that he stuck around when I was little. It was the Depression. Mom kicked him out. Other people's fathers disappeared when they couldn't support their families. They hit the road.

Not my dad. Even though Mom wouldn't let him visit, he'd wait for me till school was out and then walk me home. It was our little secret. Then, when I was sixteen, I got married. My husband was transferred out west and I hardly ever saw Dad after that. I was busy raising my own family. I did see him one Christmas when we went home, but so much was going on. You know how it is with holidays.

There was one moment I'll never forget. We were in the car together, going to pick up some groceries, stopped at a red light. I opened my mouth to say how I felt about him. He was looking right at me. But all of a sudden, I felt so shy, and then the light changed. The moment was gone. Dad died the following spring. I never got another chance.

Mildred Potter managed to push herself through many shy silences in the years after she discovered the cost of reticence. By the time she reached her seventies, she was known as someone who spoke her mind at every opportunity.

Keep up the fight.

BURT SMITH

Age 70

*Y*ou know what I wish? That I could have lived openly as a gay man. Even now, I'm afraid of the cleaning lady finding out. It's one thing to be hated out in the world and another to be hated in your own home.

My generation spent our whole lives in hiding. We lost jobs, we covered up by getting married, we denied who we were. Forgive us if we're not especially trusting or secure. We have a highly developed radar for who hates us, who seems to tolerate us, and who actually allows for the possibility of our existence.

Yes, times have changed. Things are better. I'll grant you that, but there's a lot of work left to do.

Burt Smith eventually got tired of hiding his sexual identity from the lady who cleaned his apartment. He decided to hang a calendar on his refrigerator that made things clear. She took one look at it and fled the scene, never to return. Burt asked me to call the agency that sent her, tell them he was gay, and ask for a worker who did not hate gay people. On the phone, the supervisor fell silent. Finally, she spoke: "Your request is fine. I'm just having trouble thinking of anyone I can send out there."

Watch out for stubborn pride.

JERRY HERSCH

Age 70

I was too good at keeping grudges. If somebody crossed me, that was it. Finished. You could get down on your knees and I wouldn't bat an eyelash. I dropped friends right and left. No one could live up to my standards. Then my daughter wrote me off. I didn't come through on a promise, and zap, she was done with me. She wouldn't let me explain. I got a taste of my own medicine. It's been more than twenty years now and we haven't said a word to each other. I've been wanting to call my daughter, but it's too late. I let too many years go by.

The approach of death sometimes dislodges longstanding obstacles. After he was told that his cancer was rapidly progressing, Jerry Hersch began talking about things he had never broached in conversation. He also
became tender, something he had been unable to be earlier in his life.
He lamented a twenty-year breach with his daughter, but was afraid to
reach out to her at the last minute. What if she didn't respond? Instead,
with the last of his strength, he gave voice to his legacy of regret.

Later Life

Growing older makes you more certain about what's meaningful.

CARTER CATLETT WILLIAMS
Age 76

*U*ntil my husband was nearing retirement, I did whatever I could to support his work. Everyone liked my food and our hospitality, but I generally kept quiet while the scientists discussed matters important to them. I knew I saw things they didn't see, but I seldom spoke up. I had no confidence that my perceptions were of value to others.

Then, when I was in my mid-sixties, I started to venture forth with my observations and raise questions few people were asking. By that time, it didn't matter to me whether others agreed with me, only that I speak the truth as I saw it.

At long last, I knew I had something to say—or rather, I knew there were things that needed to be said and I had to join the few who were saying them.

In the 1980s, Carter Catlett Williams became a national leader in the effort to stop the practice of restraining nursing home residents by tying them to chairs or binding their bodies to beds and side rails. She spoke up on behalf of people who were unable to command the attention of lawmakers and regulators, until restraint-free care became the law of the land. Lack of confidence, which had restrained Carter since she had come of age, finally receded as she found her voice in later life.

Firm convictions are easiest to maintain when you're young.

HELMUT MAYER
Age 68

Show me someone getting on in years and I'll show you someone who doesn't have a lot of answers. Don't ask me what life is for. I haven't figured it out yet. I used to know, or I thought I did.

Early on, you think just because something seems a certain way to you, that's how it is. Case closed. But as you get older, how many times are you sure of something and then it turns out you were dead wrong?

Young people often think the old are set in their ways, but that's just on the surface, just a bunch of petty habits and the like. Old people are actually the open-minded ones.

While enduring respiratory illness, Helmut Mayer taught himself to use a word processor and dedicated himself to writing the narrative of his early life in Germany. Near the end of the war, the German army resorted to drafting younger and younger boys, and Helmut became a bewildered soldier at the age of sixteen. He had an intense fear of heights, but Helmut found himself in the glider airplane division. He was taught the basics of flying, and then summarily pushed off a cliff. He wrote in his memoir that despite his fear, he was overwhelmed by the silence and beauty of flight.

Old people are just people who have been around awhile.

VIOLA BURNS

Age 97

I t's terrible to be disguised as a little old lady. Young people treat me like I'm a creature from another planet. I'm as feisty as ever, and you bet I know which end is up, but fifteen-year-old kids talk down to me. Can you beat that?

Being old doesn't make a damn bit of difference. I've gotten a little smaller and gained a few more wrinkles, but I'm the same person I've always been.

Viola Burns refused to leave her downtown apartment unless she had on an attractive dress, high heels, and makeup. I advised her to forgo those particular shoes, citing the large number of people in nursing homes who are there because of broken hips from falls. She replied, "A lady is never seen in public without her heels."

Life humbles you.

NYLES GUNDERSON

Age 99

When you're young, you don't realize what you're up against. You think all those grown-ups sure have compromised. They definitely don't know how to live right. You swear there's no way you'll ever be like that. No way.

Then it starts. You run into some bad luck. Even good luck can get you stuck in a certain direction. The years go by. You find things out. Some of your best-laid plans go bust.

Pretty soon, there comes a day when some young guy with a chip on his shoulder gives you that look. He's swearing to himself never to be like you. You see it in his eyes. That's how it goes. He won't understand till his time comes.

As a young man, Nyles Gunderson earned his living as a logger but wanted to be a poet. This was in the days when crews went out with twelve-foot saws and took down huge cedar and spruce trees by hand. At night, under the stars, Nyles composed his poems and hid them away. Then came chain saws, logging trucks, and Nyles' middle age. He supported his wife and six children hauling logs with his own truck. Between all those runs back and forth to the lumber mill, poetry got lost.

Being old lets you see more of the details.

TERRY CAIN

Age 79

When you're young, you've got too much going on. There's no way to comprehend it all. Everything is coming at you at once. Life is a blur. There's an awful lot you don't appreciate about your experiences, and especially about other people. There's just too much to take in.

Gradually things settle down. You're less distracted. You're finally able to decide where to focus your attention. You start to pin things down and take a good look at them. That's when you can really see what's going on.

Terry Cain was in the Navy during World War II, but she was confined to a desk job instead of seeing the world aboard ship. Later in life she got to tour most of Europe by bicycle. Today she resides in an assisted-living facility overlooking a busy harbor, feeling as if she's in a ship that never leaves the dock.

Don't hide your age.

HENRY HORTON
Age 90

oo many people try to pretend they're younger than they are. That's ridiculous, like an elephant trying to hide behind a lamppost. Everyone sees what you're doing. Trying to hide your age only gives people cause to treat you like the fool you're being.

If you have length of days, be proud of it. Women, let those wrinkles see the light of day. Stop coloring your hair. I say, hold your head high.

Henry Horton admitted that men have it easier than women with words like "distinguished" attached to their graying temples, while women must endure words like "old hag" and "biddy." But he insisted that all men and women over a certain age must oppose our society's disparagement through defiant pride.

When you've got no other choice, that's when you change.

MAX HASTINGS

Age 89

When you're old, you've run out of time for excuses. First, I had to quit drinking. My liver was giving out. Then I had to give up my house. My legs couldn't navigate the stairs. Next, I had to go live with a bunch of biddies with poofy hair. I couldn't manage on my own. Humiliating is what it was, every last bit of it.

The strangest thing is, I'm happier than I've ever been. My son says he likes his sober father. The biddies keep bringing me pies, and they flock around me down at the mailboxes. I may not be such a bad fellow after all.

Max Hastings had been a sea captain in the merchant marine for al-
most fifty years when illness forced his retirement. At first, having to stay
on shore left him longing for his many lost freedoms. He was fond of
saying, "There's nothing like the company of men in a bar." But a new
kind of life awaited him.

Get out there and keep moving.

EDNA HARRIS

Age 79

I'm the oldest person in my hiking group by eighteen years. There's no secret to it: the reason I can walk uphill six miles at my age is because I've never stopped hiking. I may be the one farthest back on the trail, but I do it.

The older you get, the more you have to push yourself, rain or shine. You can't afford to cut yourself any slack. When I *did* stop hiking once for three weeks, it took me months to get myself back in shape. I felt like an old lady. I had lost so much ground, so quickly, it scared the daylights out of me.

Who on earth would want to tramp around in the mud instead of pulling up the covers on a rainy day and staying in bed with a hot cup of tea? I can come up with excuses like the best of them. But if I do, I know I'll turn into an old lady in three weeks flat.

I met Edna Harris on a thirty-four-mile hike in an area of New Zealand called the Milford Track. Only thirty people per day are allowed to enter this pristine region, and each day hikers must proceed on to the next shelter about ten miles away. On the trail, Edna was often the last of the thirty laboring up some of the most difficult slopes, but she always had a smile on her face. She'd get into her bunk the minute she finished dinner and fall into an exhausted sleep.

Don't be tiresome.

JENNY FLEISCHMAN

Age 98

I listen to so many old people complaining. Good night! They say the same things over and over again. Sure, there are things I'm not happy about, but I don't keep talking about them.

I've learned from observing other people my age what *not* to do. A friend calls me every night to tell me what his pain is and what awful things he's been served for dinner. In my building, I see people hunched over, inching down the hallways with frightened little steps. I force myself to stand up straight and take long strides, and every day I make sure I go up and down a flight of steps at least once, to keep my muscles limber.

Of course, there were some things I had to stop doing by the time I turned ninety. But when I find my body can't do something anymore, I accept it. I don't whine about it.

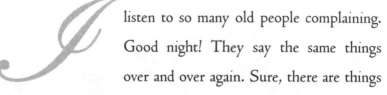

Jenny Fleischman has made a study of almost every aspect of how she sees older people walking, talking, and living out their days. Her senior apartment building has become her laboratory for experimenting with the best possible responses to aging and casting off the worst.

Life gets better as you get older.

LARRY MEYER

Age 72

Young people think they have it over us old people, but they've got it backwards. They run faster and have more hair, but that's about all the advantages right there.

In my opinion—and my friends agree—life gets easier every year. By now, we've figured out who we are. We've stopped comparing ourselves to everyone else. Best of all, we laugh at ourselves. We've finally realized that none of us really knows what we're doing. We just do the best we can.

Sure, my knees ache, but I take things easier all around, and that gives me a big lift. I wouldn't want to be young again for anything in the world.

When Larry Meyer finished high school, his family had no money to send him to college. He got a job cleaning office buildings at night, and during the day he gave himself an education through diligent reading at the public library. He became the manager of a janitorial service and went on being an avid reader all his working life. Now he serves as a volunteer ombudsman, visiting two nursing homes each week and making sure the residents there get decent care.

All that matters in the end is that you are loved.

EDNA WHITMAN CHITTICK

Age 101

*Y*ou spend half your life worrying about things that won't concern you in the slightest at the end. When you're lying in bed dying, you want people to sit by your side. That's it.

It's easy to get tricked by dreams of money and success, but all the money in the world doesn't buy you kindness. You get that because you gave it.

Every Saturday, I would read poetry to Edna Whitman Chittick. This weekly ritual was the best part of both our weeks for most of a three-year period. When her last illness was upon her, she forced her breath through an excess of water in her lungs, trying to make it through a few days until Saturday. She did, dying a few minutes after I left her room.

Author's Note

Asking older people what they have learned from experience is an act of respect. Sadly, many of our elders have so absorbed the prevailing scorn for aging that they do not feel worthy of being asked. Some insist that they have nothing special to say. Others will offer quick platitudes instead of reaching deeply inside themselves for their distinctive perceptions.

I have found that it helps to have questions at hand that convey both need and hope—the need for special insight about what it means to live well, and the hope of using such wisdom to make a better life for the questioner. Here are some of the questions I use.

- "What do you know now that you wish you'd known when you were young?"
- "What advice would you give a young person just starting out in life?"

- "Has anyone in your life taught you a valuable lesson? What was that lesson?"
- "If you could live your life over again, what would you do differently? What would you keep the same?"

Asking these questions because you genuinely care about the answers may lead you to much more that is worth knowing. The more heartfelt your interest in what someone has to say, the better the responses you will receive. If you happen to come across a gem not already contained in these pages, I'd love to hear it. Please feel free to send me a summary by old-fashioned mail.

Wendy Lustbader
P.O. Box 22956
Seattle, WA 98122-0956

Index by Title

On Living Well

You don't need much, *Irma Delehanty,* 1 0 • You've got to keep a sense of humor, *Rosie Barlow Mills,* 1 2 • Kindness is never wasted, *Agnes McDougal,* 1 4 • Happiness is in the smallest things, *Bernice Miller,* 1 6 • Learn to like your own company, *Annie Bakersmith,* 1 8 • Things you buy won't make you happy, *Maxine Dougherty,* 2 0 • There's always something to see if you keep your eyes open, *Lila Lane,* 2 2 • Be good to your parents—someday you may understand them, *Jack Melnick,* 2 4 • Make sure you go to Paris, *Betty Seville,* 2 6 • Don't let doubt in yourself defeat you, *Rocky Adams,* 2 8

On People

All that matters is whether someone is a good person, *Israel Grosskopf,* 3 2 • Everyone needs a little praise, *Harry McIntosh,* 3 4 • No one's better than you, and you're not better than anyone, *Agnes Wilson,* 3 6 • A good listener is someone who's not talking, *Harold Jones,* 3 8 • Fools are in this world to make us grow, *Christina Martinez,* 4 0 • It's not going to get better until we stop passing it back and forth, *Gladys Kennebrew,* 4 2 • Take care of yourself, because no one else will, *George W. Hindels,* 4 4 • Remember that flesh is weak, *Irene Munkberg,* 4 6 • Living things need lots of attention, *Giuseppe Maestriami,* 4 8 • Good fortune is having good friends, *John Caughlan,* 5 0

240

On Regret

Everyone misses out on something, *Paul Stier*, 198 • If you really want to do something, don't let yourself off the hook, *Matilda Johansen*, 200 • Beware of your prejudices—the life you condemn may be your own, *Jim Wentworth*, 202 • Learn how to speak up for yourself, *Hiroko Tomita*, 204 • The vessel that carries your spirit is fragile, *Shelby Johnson*, 206 • Say what you have to say, before it's too late, *Mildred Potter*, 208 • Keep up the fight, *Burt Smith*, 210 • Watch out for stubborn pride, *Jerry Hersch*, 212

On Later Life

Growing older makes you more certain about what's meaningful, *Carter Catlett Williams*, 216 • Firm convictions are easiest to maintain when you're young, *Helmut Mayer*, 218 • Old people are just people who have been around awhile, *Viola Burns*, 220 • Life humbles you, *Nyles Gunderson*, 222 • Being old lets you see more of the details, *Terry Cain*, 224 • Don't hide your age, *Henry Horton*, 226 • When you've got no other choice, that's when you change, *Max Hastings*, 228 • Get out there and keep moving, *Edna Harris*, 230 • Don't be tiresome, *Jenny Fleischman*, 232 • Life gets better as you get older, *Larry Meyer*, 234 • All that matters in the end is that you are loved, *Edna Whitman Chittick*, 236

About the Author

Wendy Lustbader is a nationally known keynote speaker on aging issues. She addresses thousands of people each year at professional conferences and gatherings of family caregivers. The author of two highly respected books in the field of aging, Lustbader has a master's degree in social work with a concentration in aging studies and is Affiliate Assistant Professor at the University of Washington's School of Social Work and a mental health counselor at the Pike Market Medical Clinic in Seattle. She serves on the board of *Generations,* a quarterly journal published by the American Society on Aging.